Lost Restaurants

OF

MEMPHIS

G. WAYNE DOWDY

AMERICAN PALATE

Published by American Palate
A Division of The History Press
Charleston, SC
www.historypress.com

First published 2019

Manufactured in the United States

ISBN 9781467142526

Library of Congress Control Number: 2019945079

Contents

CONTENTS

Author's Note

Restaurants are a fascinating way to explore the culture of a community. The food that people eat and the places in which they consume that food tell us so much about the character of a place and can help us understand its history. This deeper understanding of the Memphis community is the ultimate purpose of this book. It is my hope that readers will not only enjoy a nostalgic trip into the past but will also learn something along the way. While I have tried to include every major restaurant that has operated in Memphis, it is possible that some are not included due to a lack of sources. I apologize if one of your favorite restaurants is not contained within these pages.

This book would not have been possible without the love and support of my family. I dedicate this book to my parents, Barbara Ann Nance and Gerald McLain Dowdy; my grandparents, John McLain and Ivy Lucile Heckle Dowdy and William Herbert and Lurline Bell Griffin Nance; my brother and sister-in-law, William Johnathan "Bud" and Robin Paige Clement Dowdy; my niece, Britney Amber Dowdy Pierce; my nephew-in-law, Larry Hank Pierce; my grand-niece, Mallorie Ann Pierce; my nephews, Cody Austin Dowdy and Brandon Ryan Dowdy; my Uncle J.B. and Aunt Carole Nance; my Uncle Larry H. Nance; my Uncle Ron G. and Aunt Donna Nance; my Aunt Viola Heckle; my cousins, Justin, Clay and Clint Nance, Lisa Nance Brooks, Mike and Forrest Brooks, Chris, Heather and Haleigh Nance, Gene and Jean Hair Miller, Laura Leigh Miller Traylor, John, Olivia Belle and Conrad Traylor, Eddie, Rachael, Alex and Stuart

Miller, Lanie and Martha Miller, Faye Stabler, Kim Hair Sox, Donald, Corey and Luke Sox, W.D. Hair, Ann and Harold Waldon, Jessica Renea Dellamano, Farah Dawn Brownlow and Evan Caruso.

I would also like to thank my colleagues in the History and Social Sciences Department at the Benjamin L. Hooks Central Library: Gina Cordell, Robert Cruthirds, Scott Healy, Verjeana Hunt, Scott Lillard, SeCoya McNeil, Leigh Ann Scarbrough, Belmar Toney and Marilyn Umfrees for their friendship and encouragement. The History Press is a wonderful publisher to write for, and I thank everyone there for their support, especially my editor, Chad Rhoad, for asking me to write this book. And, last but not least, my love goes out to Gina Cordell, Paul Gahn, my godson, Ellis Nelson Cordell Gahn, and Carey, Beena, Natacha, Mischa, Dennis White, Derrick E. Patterson and Peyton Dubose.

1

"His Table Will Always Be Well Supplied"

I n 1819, when Memphis was founded, the only place residents and travelers could purchase a meal was the home of Patrick "Paddy" Meagher. An early settler, Meagher eked out a living by providing food, shelter and firewood to riverboats and their workers. In 1826, Meagher opened the Bell Tavern, a ramshackle structure located on the east side of Front Street. Not long after the Bell Tavern opened, R.H. Wynne opened the Jackson Hotel, and in March 1828, Joseph Kerr opened an inn and boardinghouse located at the "sign of the cross keys, near the landing at the mouth of Wolf River." In a newspaper advertisement from May 3, 1828, Kerr stated that his boardinghouse "is not of an inviting appearance, but his table will always be well supplied." These nascent restaurants were soon joined by Anderson's Hotel. On January 13, 1828, Frances Trollope, mother of famed British novelist Anthony Trollope, visited Memphis, where she ate and slept at Anderson's Hotel. Later, she described a typical Memphis dining experience in her book *Domestic Manners of the Americans*:

> When the great bell was sounded from an upper window of the house, we proceeded to the dining room. The table was laid for fifty persons and was already nearly full....We were told that since the erection of this hotel, it has been the custom for all the male inhabitants of the town to dine and breakfast there. They ate in perfect silence, and with such astonishing rapidity that their dinner was over literally before ours was begun; the instant they ceased to eat, they darted from the table in the same moody

silence which they had preserved since they entered the room, and a second set took their places, who performed their silent parts in the same manner. The only sounds heard were those produced by the knives and forks.

THE GAYOSO HOUSE

On April 20, 1807, Robertson Topp was born to John and Comfort Topp, who lived near the Tennessee state capital of Nashville. As a teenager, Robertson studied law in his brother John's office and, once deemed qualified, practiced law in Columbia until he moved to Memphis in January 1831. Quickly becoming one of the city's most respected attorneys, Topp began investing in land just south of the Memphis city limits. He also entered politics—in 1835, he was elected to the Tennessee General Assembly, where he served until 1837. In the same year as his election, he married Elizabeth Vance, and they eventually had eight children. In addition to his political career and real estate holdings, Robertson Topp also worked tirelessly to build the Memphis & Ohio Railroad and served as an officer in the Mexican-American War.

When he returned to Memphis after the end of the 1837 session, Topp focused on developing his real estate holdings on the southern fringe of the city. The following year, a real estate firm headed by Topp purchased an additional 414 acres, built streets and sold lots. According to Memphis historian Paul Coppock, the "company laid off Shelby Street, an extension of Front Row in Memphis, and Main [Street], which continued the Memphis street. [The] principal residential streets were Beal, then spelled without the final 'E'; Linden, named after a grove of trees; and Vance, for Mrs. Topp's family." Near Beal, Topp built a beautiful mansion before turning his attention to constructing a showplace that would draw businesses and residents to what was beginning to be referred to as South Memphis.

In order to draw more attention to South Memphis, Topp laid the foundation for a grand hotel located on Front Street. Completed the following year, the hotel was named for the former Spanish governor of the Memphis region, Don Manuel Gayoso de Lemos. The Gayoso House provided not only opulent rooms for guests, such as Kentucky senator Henry Clay and Vice President John C. Calhoun, but also fine dining in a rough-hewn city populated by 2,200 people. The popularity of the Gayoso House brought many well-heeled Memphians to the southern outskirts, and some even built lavish homes like Topp's stately mansion. The amount of wealth

Built by Robertson Topp, the Gayoso House was named for the former Spanish governor of the Memphis region, Don Manuel Gayoso de Lemos. *Courtesy of the Memphis and Shelby County Room, Memphis Public Libraries.*

and political power concentrated in the area soon led to South Memphis being incorporated into a separate municipality on January 6, 1846. Despite the popularity of the Gayoso House, South Memphis did not expand economically, and in 1850, it merged with its larger neighbor, Memphis. Their customers sat at long tables, elbowing each other for access to the piles of food. The Gayoso House operated in much the same way until after the Civil War, when it became standard for restaurants to offer expanded hours and private tables.

Meanwhile, several other restaurants, aside from the Gayoso House, operated in Memphis, including the Belvidere House, which was owned by H.E. Hezekiah and opened in 1849. Located on Washington Street, the Belvidere House promised that its "bar [was] furnished with the best liquors, and customers [would] be furnished in 'double quick time' with such delicacies as oysters, fresh fish, venison, ham and eggs–birds, etc….served up in any style required." The Empire House, Green Tree Coffee House, O'Hanlon's Exchange, Rialto Restaurant and White House all offered similar fare: fish, oysters, squirrels and other wild game. Meals were only available at certain hours; for example, Gasper Fransioli's Memphis Coffee House on Front Row served lunch six days a week from 10:00 a.m. to noon.

In 1861, the State of Tennessee left the United States and, shortly thereafter, joined with other commonwealths in a Southern Confederacy. This secession led to the Civil War, which laid waste to much of the South and ended the scourge of slavery. Although a slave owner and native Southerner, Robertson Topp refused to serve the Confederate States, and when Memphis fell to Union forces in June 1862, he continued in his neutral stance. However, many United States officers stayed at his hotel and often enjoyed its table.

The only other military action Memphis experienced during the Civil War occurred in 1864, and the Gayoso House played a major role in the skirmish. On August 21, Confederate cavalry under the command of General Nathan Bedford Forrest stormed into Memphis to capture high-ranking Union generals and release Confederate POWs that were being held in Irving Block Prison. Hoping to capture Major General Stephen Hurlburt, Captain William Forrest, the commander's brother, rode into the lobby of the Gayoso House and demanded the desk clerk produce him. Unfortunately for Captain Forrest, the general was staying at the home of a comrade. The raid had absolutely no strategic importance, but it did provide a favorite Memphis story that continued to be told well into the twenty-first century.

Despite the economic challenges faced by the United States during the Civil War, Memphis was booming in 1864. Nothing is more indicative of this than the Christmas Day menu that was offered at the Gayoso House that year. The bill of fare began with oyster soup, broiled whitefish, baked bass, fried, raw and pickled oysters and escalope, au gratin, stewed in champagne, jelly and fine herbs. The meal continued with boiled ham, chicken, tongue, roast beef, turkey and a ladle of mutton. Cold ornamental dishes included boned capon decorated with jelly, ornamented ham sursackel à la Cologne and venison pie on pedestal a la Strasbourg. Among the entrées were calf's head fricasseed à la financière, fillet of trout larder à la mareshal and salmi of domestic ducks potted à la compote. The vegetables offered were cabbage, fried parsnips, mashed potatoes, rice, small onions and tomatoes. The desserts included cherry pie, English plum pudding, fresh peach meringue, strawberry pie and vanilla Charlotte Russe.

When the war ended, the hotel portion of the Gayoso House faced increased competition from newer establishments, but Memphians still regularly dined at its elaborate table. By the summer of 1876, the health of its founder, Robertson Topp, began to fail, and he died on June 13. According to the *Daily Appeal*, the news "came upon the city like the shadow of a great

DINNER.

❋

Celery

SOUP.

Scotch Broth   Consomme, Jardiniere

Olives   Sliced Tomatoes   Sliced Cucumbers   Chow Chow   Sweet Gherkins

FISH

Boiled Red Snapper, Egg Sauce
Potatoes, Naturel

Roast Ribs of Beef, au Jus

Boiled Potatoes   Boiled Onions   Cauliflower

Roast Spring Lamb, Mint Sauce

Mashed Potatoes   Snap Beans

Roast Short Ribs of Beef, with Browned Potatoes

Cutlets of Sweetbreads, Sauce Supreme

Macaroni, a la Italienne

CHARTREUSE PUNCH
Lady Fingers

Roast Turkey, Cranberry Sauce
Candied Yams

Lobster Salad

Cottage Pudding, Fruit Sauce
Damien Capriz

Assorted Cakes   Vanilla Ice Cream

Fruit   Nuts   Raisins

Roquefort, Edam and Fromage de Brie Cheese
Water Crackers

Coffee

Breakfast, 6:30 to 11:00   Luncheon, 1 to 2:30   Dinner, 6:00 to 8:30

All Dishes Ordered, Not on Bill of Fare will be Charged Extra.

GAYOSO HOTEL,
MEMPHIS, TENN.
OCTOBER 18, 1897

GEO. McGINLY,
PROPRIETOR. ✓

TRACY PRINT. CO.

A Gayoso House menu from October 18, 1897. *Courtesy of the Memphis and Shelby County Room, Memphis Public Libraries.*

cloud." The newspaper went on to praise Topp as "one of the oldest, ablest, and most useful citizens of Memphis." Meanwhile, his restaurant continued to offer some of the best food in Memphis. For example, its menu for Friday October 14, 1887, included:

Chicken Consommé with Okra
Boiled Red Snapper in Oyster Sauce
Boiled St. Clair Bacon and Turnip Greens
Leg of Mutton in Caper Sauce

Choice of:
Chicken Fricassee with Dumplings
Pig's Feet, Crumbed
Veal Kidneys
Macedoine of Fruit à la Chantilly

Choice of:
Sirloin of Prime Beef
Tennessee Short Ribs
Breast of Veal, Stuffed
Romain Punch
Young Shaker Turkey, Cranberry Sauce
Potatoes, Boiled or Mashed
Candied Sweet Potatoes
Okra
Fried Egg Plant
Pickled Beets
Hominy
Rice

Choice of:
Fruit Pudding
Green Apple Pie
Gayoso Cream Pie
Angel Food
Vanilla Ice Cream

The building, however, continued to deteriorate, and on July 4, 1899, it burned to the ground after a group of boys threw firecrackers into a nearby cotton warehouse. Robertson Topp's Gayoso House brought fine dining and elegance to a city not used to either. By the time it finally closed, the Gayoso had greatly contributed to the growth of Memphis's restaurant industry.

THE PRINCE OF MEMPHIS RESTAURATEURS

Perhaps the greatest restaurateur in nineteenth-century Memphis was a French immigrant who trained in one of the country's most famous eating establishments. Born on a small, impoverished farm in Aveyron, France, on January 4, 1828, Jean Gaston relocated to Paris when he was twelve years old to work in his uncle's restaurant. Gaston learned all aspects of the food preparation business and later went to work as a steward on an ocean liner that sailed regularly between Le Havre and New York. In 1849, Gaston arrived in New York, where he discovered a restaurant advertising French cuisine. Intrigued, he dined at Delmonico's before his scheduled return to Le Havre. Gaston was so impressed with the atmosphere and fine food that he quit his job and went to work in America's finest restaurant.

Giovanni Del-Monico, a native of Ticino, Switzerland, opened a pastry shop in lower Manhattan that sold coffee, European desserts, ices and wine. Anglicizing his name to John Delmonico, he and his brother, Peter, opened a restaurant that quickly became the most famous eating establishment in New York City and the United States. As we have seen, most eating establishments only provided hot food during limited hours, but when Delmonico's started to provide prepared dishes throughout the day at private dining tables, other restaurants soon followed suit. According to food historian John Mariani, when customers arrived at Delmonico's, they were presented with "a seven-page *Carte du Restaurant Francais* printed in both French and English.…[It offered] nine soups, eight side dishes, fifteen seafood preparations, eleven beef items, twenty kinds of veal, eighteen vegetables, sixteen pastries, thirteen fruit dishes, and sixty-two imported wines." Historian Louise Gambill also wrote that Delmonico's "not only introduced European dishes, but cooked American foods in new ways, making greater use of vegetables and adding salads to the menu." During the two years Gaston worked at Delmonico's, he learned not only how to prepare French and American cuisine but he also learned about presentation and customer service—knowledge that would serve him well when he finally made his way to Memphis.

Gaston arrived in the Bluff City in 1865 after working in several Florida and Georgia hotels and serving in the Confederate army, where he wounded his shoulder. Like many in the South, the Civil War left Gaston with little to his name, so, when he landed in Memphis, he had no money and only a few possessions wrapped in a bundle. Fortunately, he became acquainted with a prosperous French hairdresser named Justine Casimir Rodner, who soon took him under his wing. While working in the garden of Rodner's stately Fort Pickering home, Gaston recovered from the war and soon began looking for a job. By the end of 1865, he had secured the position of meat cook at the Golden Eagle Restaurant, located at 20 Madison Avenue and owned by Edward Doutaz. Gaston worked hard as a cook, saving most of his wages to purchase his own restaurant. Gaston would often say, "When you make a dollar, save it. Someday you'll have a use for it." It did not take long for the meat cook to find use for his savings—in 1867, he pooled his resources together and opened the Commercial Restaurant at 44 Adams, next to a fire station near the city's growing business district.

When he opened his restaurant there were twenty other eateries operating in Memphis. These included the Nonpareil Saloon and Restaurant at the corner of Madison and Monroe Avenues, the Planter's Restaurant on Monroe Avenue, Sam's House at 58 Jefferson Avenue, the Senate Restaurant on North Court Avenue and the Great Republic Restaurant at 83½ DeSoto Street, which catered to African Americans. The Commercial Restaurant was a small establishment with rooms for rent on the second floor. Despite the restaurant's small size, its location made it a popular destination and afforded Gaston the opportunity to experiment with his menu and save money for expansion. In 1871, Gaston used the money he earned at the Commercial to build a much grander restaurant across from Court Square at 33–35 Court Avenue. In this new restaurant, Gaston did for Memphis what Delmonico's did for New York—he combined European and American cooking to create new dishes that were both exciting and palatable. Meals cost fifty cents, which was within the budget of some skilled workers and professionals. Gaston soon became the city's most respected restaurant owner; the *Memphis Appeal* newspaper referred to him as "the prince of Memphis Restaurateurs."

When a male customer arrived at Gaston's—at that time, custom continued to prevent most women from eating in public—they were ushered into the dining room by African American waiters who provided them with that day's menu. If a customer was not attired in his own coat, he was strongly urged to choose from the establishment's collection. This

John Gaston trained at
Delmonico's in New York
City before opening a French
restaurant in Memphis.
*Courtesy of the Memphis and
Shelby County Room, Memphis
Public Libraries.*

did not mean that all diners took the hint. Once, an engineer arrived for dinner in a dirty shirt. When he refused to put on an offered coat, Gaston charged him $1.50 for his meal. Although he paid up, the soiled engineer sent Gaston collect telegrams that stated, "Mr. John Gaston. Don't you think $1.50 was too much for that meal?" Obliged to accept the telegrams because they might contain legitimate business, Gaston paid for each one. In addition, no dogs were allowed in the dining room and customers were prevented from smoking.

In his later years, Gaston devoted much of his time to civic affairs; he was a member of the Business Men's Club, the Elks and the Industrial League. He was also a very active member of Calvary Episcopal Church. In 1900, he donated five acres of land for a city park, and after his death in 1912, his estate funded additional land for a community center in Gaston Park and a hospital that was also named for the famed restaurateur. Gaston's Restaurant did not survive its owner's passing, but the name John Gaston remains a respected one in Memphis.

GRAND DUKE ALEXEI

In 1871, President Ulysses S. Grant invited the twenty-two-year-old son of the Russian czar, Alexander II, to tour the United States. Arriving in November, Grand Duke Alexei conferred with President Grant at the White House, visited the eastern United States and hunted bison with Buffalo Bill Cody in Nebraska. His party then made their way to the American South. Icy rain fell as the train bearing Alexei and his escort, Lieutenant Colonel George Armstrong Custer, arrived at the Memphis and Ohio Railroad Depot on February 2, 1872. Despite the inclement weather, a large crowd gathered to gawk and cheer the Russian noble as he boarded a carriage and was whisked to the Peabody Hotel.

The hotel was built by Robert C. Brinkley, a prominent lawyer who had come to Memphis in 1842 from middle Tennessee. Originally called the Brinkley House, the name was changed when Brinkley had a chance encounter with noted banker and philanthropist George Foster Peabody while visiting London. Brinkley was so impressed with his new friend that he became determined to name his new hotel in Peabody's honor. Opened on February 6, 1869, the hotel was soon known for its well-stocked restaurant. According to one newspaper account, the "dining [was] a perfect paragon of beauty, which [was] presided over by the most affable steward, and a corps of thoroughly trained waiters."

After meeting Mayor John Johnson, former Confederate States president Jefferson Davis and other local dignitaries, the duke retired to his private suites until 6:30 p.m., when he and his entourage walked into the Peabody's lavish dining room. The room was draped in red, white and blue bunting, evergreen boughs and the flags of Imperial Russia and the United States. Taking their seats, the grand duke and his guests proceeded to partake in what was perhaps the greatest meal served in Memphis during the nineteenth century. The courses were:

Relish—Oysters on the half shell
Soup—Chicken gumbo
Fish—Broiled lake trout, sauce remoulade
Boiled—Chicken with pork, leg of mutton, caper sauce
Relevé—Boned turkey sauté; tongue aspick à la Chartreuse; pate of hare, à la Strasbourg
Entrees—Fillet of beef larded, sauce tomat; quail au fumé a l'impérial; chicken sauté à la Marengo; salmi of ducks à la Monarchie; baked macaroni au gratin

Roast—beef; turkey, aux truffles
Game—Saddle of venison with cranberry sauce; prairie chicken with
    currant jelly
Vegetables—Mashed Irish potatoes; green beans; hominy; stewed
    tomatoes; spinach; rice; celery; asparagus
Pastry—Cabinet pudding, wine sauce; chocolate kisses; madeleines;
    vanilla ice cream; coconut custard pie; Rhine wine jelly à la Française;
    mince pie
Dessert—Bananas; raisins; figs; filberts; pecans; oranges; almonds;
    French coffee; English walnuts; Malaga grapes

Before retiring to his rooms at the Peabody, Alexei attended a formal ball at the nearby Overton Hotel, where he danced the Lancers and other popular steps. He remained in Memphis until Monday, February 5, when he left for New Orleans. The visit of the grand duke was not only the social highlight of the century but it also expanded the city's restaurant industry and established Memphis as an important American culinary center.

LUERMANN'S

Second only to John Gaston in the realm of famous nineteenth-century restaurateurs was Henry Luermann. Born in 1841 in the Hanover region of what would become Germany, Leurmann immigrated to St. Louis at the age of fifteen and worked as a clerk while studying business at night. He served in the Union army during the Civil War, and after he was mustered out in 1864, he worked as a civilian clerk to a cavalry unit stationed in Memphis. After the war, he briefly returned to St. Louis before permanently relocating to the Bluff City in 1866, where he secured a position as clerk at the Sweisfel and Hergen brewing company. A few years later, Luermann managed the V. Dreisigaker Saloon on Monroe, where he constructed a beer bottling plant next door. He soon became the official bottler for the Jos. Schlitz Brewing Company. Barrels of beer would arrive by railcar from Milwaukee, and Luermann would store them under tons of ice. His staff would then bottle the beer and sell it in his saloon. He had room in the bottling plant for four hundred barrels, and he later built the first cold storage plant in the South.

Over time, Luermann expanded his business to include catering food for banquets. In 1883, he abandoned beer and opened the Terrace Garden restaurant at the corner of Monroe and Main Streets. Luermann's cuisine was unique because it was composed of German food rather than the traditional French dishes that were offered at Gaston's and the Peabody. Like other restaurateurs, Luermann added a hotel to the Terrace Garden, but it was destroyed by fire in 1892. Undeterred by this disaster, Luermann built a grander hotel and restaurant on the other side of Monroe Avenue at 296 Main Street. This location became the most celebrated restaurant in Memphis during the Gilded Age. Some of its most popular entrées included canvasback duck shipped from Michigan, South American partridges, turkey wings with rice and jelly, shrimp and oyster omelet and chicken livers en brochette. Guests at Luermann's table included the cream of Memphis society as well as noted actors Minnie Madden Fiske and Nat Goodwin and famous businessman and philanthropist Diamond Jim Brady.

According to one of the restaurant's African American waiters, John Brame, the owner's attention to detail was legendary: "First thing Mr. Luermann would do when he came into the hotel every morning would be look over the bar. It was his pride. Every glass must be shining, and the brass

Henry Leurmann's restaurant was the most celebrated in Memphis during the Gilded Age. *Courtesy of the Memphis and Shelby County Room, Memphis Public Libraries.*

must be polished....After he inspected the bar, it was his habit to walk into the dining room and sit down at his table, when a waiter would bring him a pot of coffee." A true connoisseur of java, Luermann would pour a small cup, pass it under his nose, and, if it didn't meet his satisfaction, he would order that the coffee be thrown out and that a new batch was to be made. Luermann kept live lobsters, oysters and crabs in the basement, where he allowed no one but himself to feed the shellfish. Brame recalled that you could hear the oysters snapping in anticipation whenever the basement door opened. "We had the best food in the country. We had 135 different kinds of wines. We specialized in steaks and seafood, had huge ammonia refrigerators with glass doors so patrons could see the food packed in ice," remembered William H. Otte, who went to work at the restaurant in 1900. Luermann's was the highest priced establishment in Memphis—Otte remembered that a sirloin steak dinner cost $1.50.

Unfortunately, things began to unravel quickly for Luermann. In 1904, the restaurant building was sold for $91,000 to pay creditors, and Luermann's health soon deteriorated. After his passing in 1905, the restaurant and hotel limped along until 1909, when it was closed in the wake of the Tennessee legislature outlawing the sale and manufacture of alcohol. On the day the restaurant closed, William Otte said he had witnessed the end of an era. "I was the last one there, watching the furniture sold at auction," he recalled.

BY THE 1890s, THE POPULATION of Memphis was 64,495, and its restaurant scene had grown from a small collection of taverns and boardinghouses to one of the South's most important dining centers. The Gayoso House, John Gaston, Henry Leurmann and the Peabody Hotel's dining room had put Memphis on the fine dining map. There were also many other restaurants that contributed to Memphis's vibrant food service culture. In 1893, there were thirty-four restaurants in Memphis, including the Fransioli Brothers, Oakey's American Kitchen and the Vienna Cafe. Most of these restaurants were located on Beale, Front and Main Streets, but others were beginning to open on Adams, Court, Poplar, Jefferson and Union Avenues. This trend of eateries opening beyond the downtown business district laid the foundation for the explosive growth of the Bluff City's restaurant industry in the twentieth century.

2

"Wonderful Food at Reasonable Prices"

With the dawn of the twentieth century, Memphis's economy grew to such an extent that more citizens could afford to eat in restaurants than ever before. The number of eateries had nearly doubled to fifty-four by 1900, and they were beginning to be established outside of the downtown business district. For example, Poplar Avenue, which was a franchise that ran east to west from the Mississippi River to well beyond the city limit, had four dining establishments, including one operated by an African American man named George Oglesby.

Until the 1900s, African Americans were prevented by custom and law from eating in Memphis's restaurants that were not specifically catered to the "colored trade." Before the turn of the century, records suggest that there was only one black restaurant in Memphis: the Great Republic Restaurant, located on DeSoto Street. However, by 1908, there were twenty-eight restaurants serving the African American community. According to Green P. Hamilton's book *The Bright Side of Memphis*, which was a "compendium of information concerning the Colored people of Memphis," Susie Ammons ran "the most popular restaurant in the middle part of Memphis, and [it had] such large patronage that it [taxed] all of her resources to cater to their wants." Hamilton's book also contains several advertisements for restaurants, including this one:

Popular Prices…Quick Service
Meet me at the Cozy Little ELITE CAFE,

Mrs. Lillie Brewer and Wm. H. Overall, Proprietors.
Up-to-date meals served at all hours. Short orders a specialty. Sandwiches of
all kinds. Open from 5:30 a.m. to 1 a.m. Give Us a Call. 73 McCall Ave.

THE GAYOSO RETURNS

It will be remembered that, in 1899, Memphis's first fine dining establishment, the Gayoso House, was destroyed by fire. A group of investors, including Memphians Jerome Hill, R.M. McLean and the president of the Illinois Central Railroad, Stuyvesant Fish, hired architect James B. Cook to design a new building. Opened on March 28, 1902, the new Gayoso House was located on South Main Street near the Goldsmith's Department Store. The new hotel included a café, which was described in a hotel brochure as the "best place in town to eat." The brochure also stated, "To this reputation no little is contributed by rich Golden Guernsey Milk, savory Hampshire sausage and dewy-fresh vegetables from the hotel's own Gayoso Farms." The main dining room was open year-round, even on major holidays. For Thanksgiving Day 1939, the Gayoso offered not only a turkey, oyster dressing and cranberry sauce entrée but also such delicacies as baked stuffed fresh lobster à la thermidor julienne, broiled sirloin steak and cold baked Virginia ham. For dessert, the Gayoso served ambrosia with fruit cake, fresh pumpkin pie and hot mince pie to its hungry diners.

In 1937, the Gayoso Coffee Shop opened in the lobby of the original hotel and restaurant, and it quickly became one of the most popular inexpensive restaurants in Memphis. Emphasizing its newly installed air conditioning system, the entrance to the coffee shop contained windows laced with snow and ice. Many patrons were impressed with the food and service, and a newspaper reporter from Mississippi wrote, "If you have been up to the Gayoso recently you will know they have established a fine-fitted restaurant on the main floor which well maintains the Gayoso's reputation for excellence of service. I went into this pleasant new eating place and a smiling waitress awaited my order." According to C.C. Cartwright, manager of the Gayoso, the staff was "trained in modern efficiency, designed to best serve the daily group of cotton men, lumbermen, lawyers, office workers, club women and shoppers who throng to the Gayoso Coffee Shop for taste treats amid cool, comfortable surroundings." Working-class people were not

Left: This postcard shows the interior of the new Gayoso House, which was built in 1902. *Courtesy of the Memphis and Shelby County Room, Memphis Public Libraries.*

Below: The Gayoso House Coffee Shop served some of the best inexpensive meals in Memphis during the late 1930s. *Courtesy of the Memphis and Shelby County Room, Memphis Public Libraries.*

the only ones who ate at the coffee shop—several prominent musicians of the 1930s partook in the Gayoso's "taste treats," including Jimmy Dorsey, Little Jack Little and Fred Waring.

A typical breakfast menu from the Gayoso Coffee Shop in the 1930s contained not only à la carte items, such as corned beef hash, fried calf brains in butter, veal cutlets and wheat cakes, but there were also three specials:

> *Number One - - 30 cents*
> *Orange juice or tomato juice or kraut juice*
> *Toast and jelly with strip of bacon*
> *Coffee, tea or milk*
>
> *Number Two - - 45 cents*
> *Choice of:*
> *Cereals, fruits in season*
> *Tomato juice or orange juice*
> *Choice of:*
> *Scrambled calf brains and eggs*
> *Chipped beef in cream*
> *Sausage, ham or bacon and eggs*
> *Waffles or cakes and bacon or sausage*
> *Toast or rolls*
> *Coffee, tea or milk*
>
> *Number Three - - 55 cents*
> *Choice of cereals or fruit in season*
> *Choice of:*
> *Spanish omelet*
> *Grilled calf's liver with bacon*
> *Eggs with bacon or ham or chicken livers*
> *Boiled salt mackerel with boiled potato*
> *Chicken, hashed in cream*
> *Hominy grits or fried potatoes*
> *Toast or rolls*
> *Coffee, tea, or milk*

In 1948, the Goldsmith's Department Store bought the Gayoso House and continued to operate the hotel and restaurant until 1962, when the space was converted into additional shopping and storage areas. Goldsmith's closed its downtown store in June 1990, and the old hotel remained vacant until 1994, when Belz Enterprises bought the property and spent $11.2 million converting the space into a 154-unit apartment complex.

BURKLE'S BAKERY

As a young man, Herman Burkle paid $300 for a bakery at 670 South Main Street in 1909, and two years later, he married Clara—the shop girl he fell in love with while making bread and pastries. In February 1936, Herman and Clara moved their bakery, Burkle's, to the corner of Cooper Street and Madison Avenue, near a bustling residential district. Over the next few years, the couple added a restaurant to the bakery, which became a landmark in midtown Memphis. In 1947, Clara and Herman retired, and their children, Herman Jr. and Ruth Burkle Lee, took over the operation. Burkle's, like a handful of other Memphis restaurants, was a place where seemingly everyone in the city stopped by at one point or another. Every once in a while, patrons could even run into a Hollywood star. In the 1960s, actor and art authority Vincent Price ate at Burkle's between his duties as the host of an art exhibition at the local Sears & Roebuck store. After four decades in the restaurant business, Ruth decided to retire, leaving Herman Jr. to run the business by himself. In the summer of 1976, Herman Jr. decided to close the iconic bakery because it was "just too much for one man, too complicated." On Saturday, July 3, the restaurant served its last meal, and on Monday, July 5, a party was held, and city council members Mike Cody and Oscar Edmonds served one thousand pieces of free coffee cake before Burkle's doors closed for the final time. "We always tried to serve a reasonably good meal at a reasonably good price," Herman Burkle Jr. stated.

ALONZO OF THE PEABODY

On September 4, 1925, Memphians dined on consomme bellevue, tomato surprise and roast chicken with chestnut dressing during the grand opening of the new Peabody Hotel, located at the corner of Union Avenue and Second Street. The hotel contained several restaurants that required a strong leader and experienced maître d' to maintain its standards of impeccable service and fine dining. The hotel found such a worker in Walter Alonzo Locke, an African American man from Cairo, Illinois, who served as the Gayoso restaurant's headwaiter for ten years before being recruited for the Peabody.

Locke oversaw the Venetian dining room and the Table d'Hotel restaurant, where patrons could order a full dinner composed of stuffed green peppers, crabmeat suédoise, fresh fruit cocktail; a choice of cream of new green peas au croutons, consomme madrilene or cold tomato bouillon in jelly cup; a fine selection of entrées, including boiled spring chicken, grilled English lamb chop, cold stuffed alligator pear, boiled fresh salmon and fried jumbo frog legs; and a choice of sweet potato pie, red cherry pie, apple pie, fruit tart or cherry pudding with custard sauce all for $1.50. When the Skyway on the hotel roof opened on January 20, 1939, Alonzo was responsible for the waiters who served the hotel's most expensive meal—it cost $6.50 and was a deluxe dinner of broiled sirloin steak with French fried potatoes, a chef's salad with French or thousand island dressing, a parfait modern or baked Alaska, assorted rolls and coffee, tea or milk.

The legendary head waiter of the Peabody, Alonzo Locke, and his staff. *Courtesy of the Memphis and Shelby County Room, Memphis Public Libraries.*

Alonzo quickly became a legend in Memphis. According to one newspaper account, "nearly everybody [knew and liked] Alonzo for his sterling qualities, and he, in turn, [knew] practically everybody in the city and their business and social connections. His memory never [failed] to recall faces, and names to accompany them." In addition to his instant recall of names and faces, Alonzo was also celebrated for the stern discipline he meted out to his waiters and the courtliness he showed his customers. When an out-of-town visitor glumly walked into the Venetian dining room at Christmastime, Alonzo had the kitchen serve him a special meal that made the visitor forget how lonely he was.

In November 1937, Eleanor Roosevelt arrived in Memphis, where she visited the city's children's hospital, toured the juvenile court, inspected a National Youth Administration art project and gave a speech at the Auditorium in which she declared: "[The] problem of unemployment is our basic economic problem. If we don't solve it for youth, we may as well say we can't continue our civilization." Before she gave her speech, Mrs. Roosevelt enjoyed a meal served by Alonzo and his staff. Alonzo later gushed to a reporter, saying, "She was so kind, so gracious, so democratic and that's the reason, I suppose, that she is the wife of the president of the United States." When the famous headwaiter died on August 3, 1947, the *Press-Scimitar* journalist Clark Porteous also gushed: "Alonzo of the Peabody, a tradition in his own time, has gone to a heavenly hotel....Alonzo of the flashing smile, the chesterfieldian courtesy, the humble yet proud demeanor—Alonzo who was a Memphis institution and one of the leading ambassadors of good will...for mankind, was 73."

FORTUNE-WARD'S

In 1883, Thomas Preston Fortune operated a drugstore in the lobby of the Gayoso House. Partnering with F.W. Ward, he moved his establishment to 9 North Main Street, across from Court Square, in 1906. Whenever concerts were performed in the park, customers would drive their buggies and carriages across the street for ice cream and soft drinks. Fortune's son, Harold, watched as customers who were unable to sit inside took their treats to their carriages to eat and drink, and this gave him an idea. After hiring a group of boys to take and deliver orders, Harold began offering curb service to customers so they would not have to leave their conveyances. Curb service

Fortune's Jungle Garden. *Courtesy of the Memphis and Shelby County Room, Memphis Public Libraries.*

became so popular that, in 1914, when Fortune-Ward's moved to Madison Avenue between Main and Second Streets, traffic jams became the norm. In 1920, hoping to relieve congestion, Harold Fortune opened a new location at Union Avenue and Somerville Street, but the traffic problems only increased. When Police Commissioner Thomas H. Allen informed Fortune in 1922 that the city commission would soon ban curb service, Harold moved his operation to Belvedere and Union and renamed it Fortune's Belvedere. The restaurant served hamburgers and hot dogs to Memphians looking for a quick meal, making it perhaps the city's first fast food establishment and one of the nation's first drive-in restaurants.

The most famous of Fortune's restaurants was the Jungle Garden, located at Union Avenue and Waldran Street behind a screen of bushes and trees, which gave customers a sense of isolation from the busy traffic that was just outside the garden's gates. The establishment lived up to its name with a tropical-themed lodge, exotic plants and baboons, bears, chimpanzees, parakeets and parrots that lived inside bamboo cages. The Jungle Lodge, which was located 250 feet from Union Avenue in a tree-shaded section of the property, contained a large picture window that overlooked a garden full of exotic plants and trees and a stream with live fish and stuffed tigers, monkeys and other wild animals. "What we want to convey is a complete feeling of relaxation back there. To make it as much like the country as possible. Everyone feels that if he could only get to the country and leave the hustle and worry of the city, he'd feel much better. We're trying to bring a little of the country right here to Union Avenue," Fortune explained.

In 1948, United Press International (UPI), a newspaper wire service, filed a story about the popularity of drive-in restaurants in Hollywood, California. The story reported that the "first drive-in recorded was a Memphis drugstore (Fortune's) who served hamburgers to lazy outdoor customers in 1923." UPI was apparently unaware that the Dallas, Texas Pig Stand barbecue restaurant—which offered a so-called Tennessee-style pork and sour relish sandwich—provided drive-in service two years earlier. However, evidence suggests that Fortune's was the first restaurant in the United States to offer curb-side service to customers in vehicles.

On May 7, 1956, Harold Fortune watched as a fire that had spread from the lodge consumed his jungle and bamboo cages—killing all the animals and exotic plants. He rebuilt the Jungle Garden and opened an even more elaborate restaurant at the corner of Winchester and Highway 51, which was called the Tropical Gardens. According to historian Michael Finger, the "Gardens were soon a'crawling with cockatoos, mynah birds, monkey-faced owls, king vultures, and all sorts of other critters. Inside the main office, two chimps named Tony and Jack entertained customers by riding scooters and even playing a piano!"

Harold Fortune died in 1963, and his restaurants did not last long beyond his death. The Jungle Garden and Tropical Gardens closed in the late 1960s when the properties were taken by the interstate highway system. As you will see, Memphis has been the home of several high-concept restaurants, but few have been as elaborate as Harold Fortune's lush oases from modern life.

BRITLING'S

In the 1920s and 1930s, blues musician Memphis Minnie paid tribute to the Bluff City's restaurant scene with her song "North Memphis Blues":

Now listen to me, good people, I don't aim to make you mad
You go to North Memphis café and get somethin' you never had
I tell all you people, you can rest and eat
Because the North Memphis café got everything that you really need

As Memphis Minnie's song suggests, the number of Memphians who ate out in the 1920s exploded. In 1925, there were 262 restaurants in Memphis and over 200 lunch stands that served short order meals in many of the neighborhoods across the city. Memphis's phenomenal growth in restaurants—the number of eateries in the city went from a mere 54 in 1900 to 462 in 1925—is a good indicator of how strong the city's economy was in the 1920s. Even during the worst year of the Great Depression, 1931–32, Memphis had 289 restaurants and lunch stands operating in the city. One of the most popular was a series of cafeterias that combined an elegant atmosphere with inexpensive food to create Memphis's first restaurant chain.

In 1918, a Birmingham department store owner named A.W.B. Johnson had a problem; his customers were constantly complaining that there were no restaurants close by that they could dine in after shopping. Sensing a business opportunity, Johnson decided to open a cafeteria on the top floor of his store. The cafeteria soon became such a nuisance for customers trying to shop that Johnson was forced to move the restaurant to a lot across the street. He selected the name Britling's after the main character in H.G. Wells's World War I novel *Mr. Britling Sees It Through*.

The New Britling

Located at Number 75 Union
Between Main and Front Streets on Union Ave.
Just Next to Malco Theatre

Britling's most popular cafeteria was located at 75 Union Avenue. *Courtesy of the Memphis and Shelby County Room, Memphis Public Libraries.*

Two years later, Johnson moved his operation to Memphis, where he opened a cafeteria at 155 Madison Avenue. Not long after, he built a second location, called Britling's No. 2, at 113 Main Street above the W.T. Grant's department store. On November 1, 1933, in the midst of the Great Depression, Britling's No. 2 reopened after an extensive renovation that was designed by architects George Mahan and Everett Woods. A colonial arch decorated the front entrance with a bright neon sign advertising Britling's fine food. According to a *Commercial Appeal* reporter, the interior included a "flight of steps covered with linoleum [that were] dark against walls of salmon gray. At the top of the stairs, mirrors [flashed] and the rugs of deep red with designs of ivory, [gave] a warm welcome." The new location was so

Above: The lush interior of the Britling's Cafeteria on Union Avenue. *Courtesy of the Memphis and Shelby County Room, Memphis Public Libraries.*

Opposite: During the 1938 Christmas season, Britling's saluted customers in its *Town Crier* publication. *Courtesy of the Memphis and Shelby County Room, Memphis Public Libraries.*

successful that Johnson closed the Madison Avenue location and laid plans to build a grander cafeteria closer to other downtown attractions.

For most Memphians of a certain age, when they think of Britling's it is the third cafeteria located at 75 Union Avenue, next to the Malco movie theater and the Cotton Exchange, that comes to mind. The restaurant was opened on August 2, 1938, after $80,000 was spent to renovate the building and add seating for 350 diners. Architect Everett Woods and Johnson rejected a traditional commercial design and, instead, built a two-story, colonial-style structure. A "typical old Southern plantation home," was how the *Press-Scimitar* newspaper described it. Noted historian Kenneth T. Jackson, who grew up in Memphis, described eating at Britling's with a friend in the 1950s: "The cafeteria offered wonderful food at reasonable prices—haddock for thirty-five cents was a treat I will never forget—and so the two of us went through the cafeteria line. After we received our bill, a waitress carried our respective trays to a table on the second-floor balcony, overlooking the large main dining area." Unlike other eating establishments that catered primarily to adults, Britling's emphasized that its restaurants were for the entire family. As one 1952 advertisement explained: "I heard

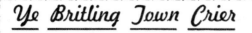

Ye Britling Town Crier

Merry Christmas
AND HAPPY NEW YEAR

To the thousands of Britling patrons we wish a Merry Christmas and a Happy New Year. Especially to their army of children who brighten the Britlings throughout the year, dining en family now so often.

To Mr. R. E. Logsdon, Director Convention Bureau, Chamber of Commerce, and Assistants a Merry Christmas and Happy New Year. Our compliments for helping make Memphis known as the Friendly City. Five hundred conventions this year — Total attendance approximately 54,000.

To Dudley D. Dumas, and the gentlemen of Cotton Row, a Merry Christmas and a Happy New Year. Our commendations to you for your outstanding work for the Cynthia Milk Fund which provides milk for thousands of Memphis needy children. May 1939 produce an abundance of "Snakes" for you. Truly yours is the Christmas Spirit that works throughout the year.

To Edward F. Barry, his associates and co-workers, a Merry Christmas and a Happy New Year. As President of the Community Fund your services have been invaluable. Our congratulations go to you for your tireless efforts in a most worthy cause.

To J. J. Brennan—familiarly known as "Joe," and to your army of Goodfellows, a Merry Christmas and a Happy New Year. Your 10th successive year as President of the Goodfellows places you in the front ranks of great workers in charitable causes. A wonderful friend of little children.

To Mr. and Mrs. H. L. Majure of Poplar Grove, Ark., Merry Christmas and Happy New Year. Our congratulations for topping the entire competition of 17,000 farm families in The Commercial Appeal-Chamber of Commerce Plant to Prosper Competition. A brilliant example of the progress being made by the farm families of Dixie.

To Clarence C. Ogilvie, Director, and to Commissioners of Goodwyn Institute Merry Christmas and Happy New Year. May we compliment you for high standard of lectures that make up the thirty-second season at Goodwyn. These free lectures contribute much to the information, inspiration and culture of the citizens of Memphis and surrounding territory.

To members of the Junior League a Merry Christmas and Happy New Year. Yours has been another year of achievement—of fine rehabilitation work, of service and care for the blind and other worthy causes.

To all other clubs, organizations and good citizens who have in any way aided in making Memphis one of the best places in the world to work and live—The Britlings salute you! Merry Christmas and a Happy New Year.

To the directors of Memphis Playgrounds—to the Parent-Teacher Associations and the other agencies helping in the welfare of the children of Memphis—a Merry Christmas and Happy New Year.

To George Eckert, president of Memphis Cotton Carnival—to its past presidents and to Mike Abt and his students, who have done such wonderful work on the floats for both the Cotton Carnival and the Spirit of Christmas Parades, a Merry Christmas and a Happy New Year.

BRITLING CAFETERIAS
155 MADISON | 75 UNION AVE.
Breakfast Served At Madison Avenue Britling Only

them say…'meet me at Britling.' Children enjoy eating at Britling. When making plans to eat at Britling, by all means, include the children." Britling's also operated cafeterias in Birmingham and Nashville, Tennessee, and Frankfort, Lexington and Louisville, Kentucky—making Memphis, for the first time in its history, the headquarters of a regional restaurant chain.

As Memphians moved eastward, away from the downtown core, in the 1950s, Britling's moved with them. In April 1956, Johnson opened a cafeteria in the city's first suburban shopping center, the Poplar Plaza, which was located at the corner of Highland and Poplar. He named this cafeteria Britling-East, and it contained three dining rooms and 245 seats, including an area that was decorated with antique guns. The cafeteria offered seven meat entrées, including corned beef, fried chicken, roast beef and turkey; eight vegetable selections; and several desserts—the most popular being chess pie, which the manager, J.J. Pratt, described as "very rich, very fattening, very nourishing and very popular." Additional cafeterias were opened in the Laurelwood and Northgate shopping centers and the Raleigh Springs Mall. Hoping to stem the eastward tide, the Madison cafeteria underwent a major renovation in 1951, which included "a smart new front combining white and veined marble with a maroon structural glass ground for enormous stainless-steel name lettering across the top." The renovation did little to improve sales, however, so, in 1956, the franchise was consolidated to its downtown location.

Britling's-Madison was closed after thirty-five years, and the Union Avenue location was remodeled for a more modern look. An additional dining room that seated 150 customers was added to the lower level, and new Danish chandeliers and colonial willow paneling were included in the main dining area. The Union Avenue cafeteria continued to thrive through the mid-1960s, but, as fewer and fewer Memphians ventured downtown, especially after the murder of Dr. Martin Luther King Jr. in April 1968, the flagship location suffered. However, by the beginning of the next decade, A.W. Boswell Johnson, son of founder A.W.B. Johnson, decided to close the gilded downtown cafeteria that was once described as a "bit of Old South" on February 1, 1971. The next day, Johnson sat in the empty dining room with *Commercial Appeal* reporter Charles Edmundson to reflect on the passing of an era. Suddenly, they heard a knock on the door. When Johnson opened it, he found a hungry farmer from Arkansas. "I'm sorry," said Johnson, "We closed this restaurant last night, after fifty years of having at least one Britling's downtown." The farmer turned away and muttered, "I've been eating at Britling's every time I came to town for twenty years." When

Britling's Madison Avenue location was in operation from 1920 to 1933. *Courtesy of the Memphis and Shelby County Room, Memphis Public Libraries.*

Johnson returned to the table, he explained in a voice tinged with pride and sadness, "Tens of thousands of mid-Southerners have come here to eat, but people, especially shoppers, don't come downtown to eat the way they used to." Britling's remained locally owned and continued to serve customers at the Poplar Plaza, Raleigh Spring and Laurelwood locations until the death of Boswell Johnson in 1979.

After Johnson's death, Britling's was sold to Blue Boar Cafeteria Company of Louisville, Kentucky, which changed the restaurant's concept. In November 1980, the Raleigh Springs cafeteria became an all-you-can-eat buffet, and the Poplar Plaza location did the same soon after. Positioning themselves as a modestly priced alternative to more expensive family restaurants, Britling's buffet cost only three dollars for lunch and one dollar more for dinner. According to the *Commercial Appeal*:

> *Diners searching for value for their food dollars would be hard-pressed to come up with anything better than Britling. The all-inclusive price includes a worthy salad bar, soup, a multitude of vegetables and entrees, hot rolls,*

beverages and a choice of six desserts. There's never a tip so the amount you pay as you enter is the true total.…With the price of a fast-food hamburger, French fries and a soft drink approaching or exceeding $3, it's easy to see the economic value of the buffet.

On a typical day's visit, diners could partake of fried okra, green beans, macaroni and cheese, mashed potatoes, turnip greens, broiled mackerel, chicken livers, fried chicken, fried fish, meatloaf, apple cobbler, chocolate pudding and ice cream. Through the 1980s, Britling's buffets remained popular, but by the early 1990s, larger restaurant chains, such as Piccadilly Cafeterias and Applebee's, had moved into the Memphis market, driving customers from the older buffets. The Poplar Plaza location closed in November 1992, and the Raleigh Springs and Laurelwood buffets shut their doors in March 1993.

THE THREE-WAY INN

Throughout the United States, hamburgers became a staple of the American diet, and Memphis was no exception. During the 1920s, hamburger stands dotted the Bluff City's landscape as Memphians satisfied their desire for a cheap, quick meal. One reason hamburger restaurants became so popular in the 1920s was that you could often get a shot of illegal booze with your sandwich. The state and federal prohibition of alcohol did little to arrest Memphians' desire for liquor. Bootleggers quickly realized that lunchrooms and small restaurants were perfect fronts for the distribution of spirits. Several eating establishments became notorious for criminal activity, including the Three-Way Inn on South Parkway that was owned by Attilio Grandi. Two of the restaurant's employees were thrown in jail when they sold liquor to an undercover police officer, and when law enforcement raided the establishment in 1925, they found twenty-three bottles of liquor and an icebox stocked with homemade beer stored under a floorboard. One evening in the fall of 1933, Attilio Grandi was forced to remove a drunk and belligerent customer named Adolph Pierotti. Not taking this very well, Pierotti returned with a knife to cut the one who insulted him. Better armed, Grandi jerked out a pistol and shot Pierotti in the legs.

ARCADE RESTAURANT

Born on the Greek island of Cephalonia, Speros J. Zepatos worked in a hotel in Athens before immigrating to Memphis to work in his uncle's bakery. A few years later, he opened the White Star restaurant but was forced to sell it when he entered the army in World War I. After he returned to Memphis in 1919, he purchased the Paris Café at 540 South Main Street, across from the central train station, and renamed it the Arcade. Business boomed in the 1920s, as train travelers stopped at the restaurant to grab a hot meal before moving down the line. The original wood frame building was torn down, and a brick structure replaced it in 1925. During World War II, Speros recalled, "I've seen the time when we would serve one thousand soldiers a day here. At times we could hardly handle them." By the time his son Harry was discharged from the military in 1955 and started working at the Arcade, train traffic was diminishing, but loyal Memphis customers continued to flock to the South Main landmark.

The restaurant successfully weathered the deterioration of downtown Memphis and was featured in Jim Jarmusch's cult film *Mystery Train* as well as the mainstream Hollywood productions *The Client* and *The Rainmaker*. Speros passed away in 1994, and a year later, Zepatos sold the business to Jacque Travis, the general manager of the Butcher Shop restaurant. Travis's tenure coincided with the beginnings of a rebirth of the South Main Historic District; newly reintroduced trolleys clanged down the street as new shops and art galleries opened in the area. Despite this, Travis was not able to keep the business going, so it was closed in December 1996. Speros's grandson, Harry Jr., "swore [he] wouldn't get back into the food business," but he hated to see his family's legacy come to an end. In March 2002, he reopened the Arcade, and it remains a Memphis landmark and popular tourist spot that has appeared on the Food Network and the Travel Channel.

LITTLE TEA SHOP

Emily A. Carpenter opened a small lunch counter at the 1918 Tri-State Fair, and it was so successful that she decided to open a restaurant. The Little Tea Shop was originally located in the basement of a building at Madison Avenue and Front Street. In 1935, Carpenter moved the restaurant to 69 Monroe Avenue, where it became a regular lunch stop for businessmen,

The Little Tea Shop was opened by Emily A. Carpenter in 1918. *Courtesy of the Memphis and Shelby County Room, Memphis Public Libraries.*

cotton speculators and government officials. One day, the president of the Cotton Exchange, C.A. Lacy, made a special request—he wanted a piece of sliced chicken placed between two cornbread sticks and smothered in gravy. The dish soon became known as the Lacy Special, and it remains on the menu to this day.

In 1946, Carpenter sold the business to amateur golfer Vernon Bell, who opened the Knickerbocker restaurant a few years later. The classic southern dishes offered by Carpenter continued under Bell, who renovated the space in 1955. Meanwhile, a young Palestinian woman named Suhair Amer arrived in Memphis with her husband, Maher, in 1967. When the couple divorced ten years later, Suhair went to work at the La Baguette bread shop, where she met businessman James P. Lauck, who asked her to manage the Little Tea Shop when he purchased it in 1982. The two eventually married, and they ran the restaurant together until his death in 2012. "Without his support and knowledge, I wouldn't be here right now. Money could not buy the wisdom I learned from this man. I went to the Jimmy school," Suhair explained.

Known to her regular customers as "Miss Sue," Suhair has become as much of an institution as her venerable restaurant. With a baseball cap perched on her head, she greets every customer with a warm smile and, like the Peabody's Alonzo Locke, remembers their names. When asked how she can cook such delicious southern dishes as chicken and dressing, fried catfish and turnip greens, Suhair replies, with a quick wit, that she is from South Jerusalem. As writer Andy Meek stated in 2018:

> *There's something distinctly Memphian about a place like this. Memphis is odd, and not in a negative sense. It's not a small town. It's not exactly a*

sprawling, cosmopolitan big city. People do their own thing here, their own way. The Little Tea Shop way includes customers filling out paper menus with stubby pencils. They flag a waitress and hand them to her, and she dutifully disappears to prepare the items they've checked off. Simple and efficient.

TODDLE HOUSE

In 1930, builder J.C. Stedman from Houston, Texas, was facing an economic conundrum—he had a great deal of lumber on his hands and nothing to build. In the hopes of staving off financial ruin, Stedman built a few small, portable houses and leased them to several local enterprises. When these businesses failed, he converted one of the buildings into a small restaurant he called Toddle House. He chose this name because the building was portable and, therefore, "toddling from place to place." Stedman wanted to build a chain of these restaurants, so he opened another Toddle House in Beaumont, but he found it difficult to build a restaurant empire in Texas.

Like so many others hoping to expand their businesses, Stedman moved to Memphis in 1932, where he leased the Toddle House franchise to a local café operator named W.W. Stevens. Less than a year later, Stevens gave up the lease and moved to Dallas, Texas, where he established his own chain of restaurants. Stedman then leased the franchise to the owner of Britling's, A.W.B. Johnson. The first Toddle House was located at 206 South Cleveland at Union, and within a short time, new restaurants were opened at Bellevue Boulevard and Madison Avenue, McLean Boulevard and Madison Avenue and Lamar Avenue at Rozelle Street. Open twenty-four hours a day, the Toddle Houses were positioned on major thoroughfares, near well-populated neighborhoods, which made them popular destinations for people heading to and from work, as well as families looking for a quick, inexpensive meal.

Each restaurant contained ten stools, a counter, a grill, a steam table and a coffee urn. They all served short order meals, such as chili, hamburgers, cheeseburgers, scrambled eggs and tenderloin steak. Toddle Houses were also unique in that customers paid their bills by placing money in a glass box on their way out the door instead of waiting for a cashier to ring them up. Robert M. Burger, one of Toddle House's general managers, described the chain as "the biggest little restaurants" in the city, and the *Press-Scimitar* agreed: "Compact, neat and equipped for quick, efficient service are the Memphis Toddle Houses. The tiny eating shops, scattered thruout [*sic*]

Left: In this publicity photo, a Toddle House waiter passes a menu to an unseen customer. *Courtesy of the Memphis and Shelby County Room, Memphis Public Libraries.*

Below: Customers enjoying sandwiches at a Memphis Toddle House. *Courtesy of the Memphis and Shelby County Room, Memphis Public Libraries.*

the city, are capable of serving their most difficult dish in ten minutes or less." In 1935, Stedman partnered with Fred Smith, the owner of the Dixie Greyhound Bus Company and father of the founder of FedEx, to form the National Toddle House Corporation.

When W.W. Stevens briefly ran the Toddle House restaurants, he added a hamburger with a slice of cheese, which he called a cheeseburger, to the menu. Stevens took the concept with him to Dallas, where, like many others, he claimed to be the originator of the cheeseburger. In 1938, Stevens put this claim to the test when he sued Toddle House and Britling's for trademark infringement. Stevens and his attorney, Sylvanus W. Polk, argued before federal judge John D. Martin that he created the cheeseburger, established the trade name by advertising the beef and dairy combination and did not give permission for Toddle House to continue offering the sandwich. Arguing for Toddle House, attorney A.L. Heiskell countered that the name "cheeseburger" had been in common use "long before Mr. Stevens claims to have originated it in 1932." As direct testimony and cross-examination droned on, Judge Martin noticed another attorney enter the courtroom. "If you stay in here, you'll get mighty hungry," the judge exclaimed as laughter interrupted the proceeding. On March 28, 1938, Judge Martin ruled that Stevens did not provide enough evidence to prove that he had exclusive rights to the tradename "cheeseburger."

A few weeks after the cheeseburger trial, Britling's announced it was severing its relationship with Toddle House. In a statement, Britling's explained, "We feel that we're in the cafeteria business and it was a little out of our line to be operating the Toddle House chain in Memphis." The ending of the relationship between the two companies did little to hurt the restaurant's bottom line. Between 1935 and 1940, the national corporation opened 100 shops in 60 major cities across the country. In their restaurants, patrons consumed 18,500 eggs, 40,400 cups of coffee, 5,000 steaks and 150,000 pieces of pie every day. In May 1940, Smith and Stedman opened their 101st restaurant at 1703 Union Avenue, east of Belvedere Boulevard—making Toddle House the most successful, locally owned chain restaurant in Bluff City history. The Toddle House also secured an honored place for Memphis in the development of the "fast food" revolution that would transform the eating habits of much of the world.

JIM'S PLACE

Nicholas (Nick) Kosta Taras left Greece in 1910, and eleven years after arriving in Memphis, he opened a café in the basement of the William Len Hotel with his partner, Jim Katsoudas, a former waiter at Johnson's Place. Nick called the café Jim's Place, and his brother George became a partner when the restaurant moved to Union Avenue and Second Street, across from the Peabody Hotel, in 1927. Taras's other brother, Bill, immigrated to Memphis and joined the business in 1935. Jim's Place's 1930s menu reflected Memphis's appetite for simple fare: broiled special Jim's club steak, broiled filet mignon, broiled T-bone steak, half spring chicken, hamburger steak made by Jim with onions and scrambled calf brains and eggs.

After World War II, Bill built a summer home on Highway 70, outside the city limits, which was a popular gathering place for the Taras family. In the 1960s, Jim's Place was relocated to Second Street, and in 1976, Bill's wife, Bessie, convinced the family to move the restaurant to their home at 5560 Shelby Oaks, off Summer Avenue. They then sold the Second Street site to Erika's German restaurant. Rechristened Jim's Place East, the menu was expanded to include Greek dishes, such as baklava and souflima, which Bill's son Dimitri explained: "[Souflima] is succulent pieces of pork tenderloin, skewered and grilled over the coals. It's a recipe that dates back to my father's days as a child in Greece."

Nick Taras passed away in 1967, and Bill continued to run the restaurant until his own death in 1988. Bill's sons, Costa and Dimitri, and their brother-in-law, Angelo Liollio, took over the business, and in 2010, they moved the restaurant to 518 Perkins Extended, near the high-traffic Poplar Avenue corridor. "We've loved being in this spot for thirty-five years, but business has changed, and we just [aren't] getting as many customers as we [need],"

Jim's Place opened on the corner of Union and Second Streets in 1927. *Courtesy of the Memphis and Shelby County Room, Memphis Public Libraries.*

stated Costa. Dimitri left Jim's Place East in 2006 to open Jim's Place Grille in the suburb of Collierville with his sons, James and Sam. Meanwhile, Jim's Place East never found its footing at the Perkins location and was forced to close in 2017. Despite this setback, the Taras family continues the traditions Nick, George and Bill began in the 1920s. As Dimitri said: "We do it all with feeling. We cook by feel, serve by feel and always try to put that extra Jim's Place personal twist on everything."

WALTON'S CAFÉ

Some of the best cooks in the Memphis region did not work on the land at all but rather on the packet boats that traveled up and down the Mississippi River. When this form of transportation declined in the 1920s, many of the chefs began working in and around Memphis. One of the most well-respected riverboat cooks was Harry H. Walton, who opened a café at 73 Monroe Avenue. The specialty of Walton's Cafe was its Club Steak Supper served with hot biscuits. "Our steaks are the choicest cuts. We leave the second quality meats for those who are not so particular. Our vegetables must be fresh and crisp. My cooks have been taught the art of cooking as it was practiced on the Mississippi River in its heyday and our customers like it," explained the café's owner. Walton also offered a free second cup of coffee, and buttered toast was provided with each meal. Cooled by several large fans, the walls of the café contained images of river packets and steamers that gave the restaurant a decidedly nautical flavor. Walton's Cafe closed around 1936, but with its riverboat décor it offered diners a unique atmosphere unlike any other restaurant in Memphis during the early 1930s.

TOPPER

Southern Foods Inc., which operated Topper Lunch Rooms on South Bellevue Boulevard and Linden Circle, leased the closed A&A Cafeteria at 119 Madison in March 1941. As their name suggests, Southern Foods wanted its white customers to enjoy a certain kind of eating experience. As the *Press-Scimitar* explained: "[The] Old South will live again in an atmosphere of magnolia trees and paintings of cotton pickers, river 'baptizings' and negro [*sic*] mammies cooking greens and vegetables when the new Topper Cafeteria opens." The president of Southern Foods, William Ross Kennedy, explained that "the cafeteria just [had] to have the mammies." On the ground floor was the Bal Masque dining room, where customers exiting the serving line found plenty of seating at bone-colored tables. Those who wanted more intimacy could walk up to the Old South Balcony, which was decorated with stagecoach lights and magnolia trees, or they could enter the nearby Natchez Room. The food operation was overseen by Chef Eddie Yingling, who had once worked at Chicago's Palmer House. On opening day, customers were given souvenir top hats, entertained by a full orchestra and were able to meet the guest of honor, Confederate general R.E. Bullington. The Topper cafeteria lasted about as long as the Confederacy—four years after its opening, the restaurant was no longer operating in Memphis.

NOTHING OVER 10 CENTS

During the worst years of the Great Depression, many restaurant owners were forced to close their doors, while others slashed prices to keep pace with the economic downturn. In the early 1930s, Olander J. Berry opened four Owl Lunch Rooms on North Dunlap, Florida Street, Union and Vollentine Avenues. Their slogan was: "nothing over ten cents." This drew frugally minded diners from the neighborhoods of South Memphis and Midtown. Hamburgers cost only five cents, and they offered "sandwiches, chili, tamales and other palatable foods that [were] comparable to the best to be had anywhere." Each café remained open until 2:00 a.m., and they delivered food to homes and businesses without charge.

By the end of the 1930s, Barry had closed his original locations and opened the Owl Cafe at 523 South Cooper Street, which became one of the city's most popular restaurants from the 1940s to the 1960s. Barry sold the café to John Gammon in the mid-1940s, and it was later bought by Clint Reeves. George Zapatos acquired the restaurant in 1957, but he was forced to close the Owl Cafe in 1962, when the building's new owner wanted to convert it to an office space. The restaurant was reopened in 1965 only to be closed for good in 1972 when the building was torn down.

Other restaurants operating in Memphis during the Great Depression included the Pit and Igloo, located at 2484 Poplar Avenue. Designed by

Boyd Ernst, the Pit offered a wide selection of sandwiches and drinks in a building reminiscent of an English manor house. Next to it was the Igloo, a frozen custard stand, which was "built of reinforced concrete over a steel frame and lined with asbestos to retain the cool air generated from the frozen custard plant." A few blocks away, on Summer Avenue, Adolph Grisanti managed the Broadway Inn. In addition to the inn's sandwiches, customers could order steaks, chicken, ravioli and spaghetti prepared by head chef Frank Benedetti. Across from the fairgrounds stood the Central-Parkway Inn, where ravioli "made in the true Italian style," spaghetti, fried spring chicken, southern pit barbecue and sandwiches were popular items on their menu. According to owner J.H. Hooker, "[We] spent years in determining just what appeals to the taste of our patrons, and we are making a sincere effort to please." As the menus of the Broadway and Central Inns suggest, Italian cuisine was becoming popular in Memphis, as were other foods that reflected Memphis's diverse culture. For example, Greek immigrant K.J. Kotsaftes operated the Klondyke Lunch Room at 1247 Jackson Avenue, and the Memphis Yiddish Restaurant at 124 South Second Street was run by Leo Largman. However, it was Chinese, Italian and Mexican cuisines that became the most popular ethnic foods in Memphis.

TAMALES WITH SOUL

Chronic labor shortages in the Arkansas and Mississippi deltas brought Chinese and Mexican workers to toil in the cotton fields with African Americans, where they shared knowledge of many things—including food. As historian Anne Martin notes: "Known simply as tamale, or tamal, the food was portable, easy to prepare and could be taken to the field." Mexican tamales are traditionally made with pork that is wrapped in seasoned corn flour dough and corn shucks. Blacks noticed how similar tamales were to the African, spicy cornmeal mush called cush. African American deltans began cooking tamales with seasoned cornmeal and different types of meat that soon spread to Memphis. Capitalizing on the dishes' popularity, in 1928, William A. Lake Sr. opened the La Rosa Tamale Company at 2581 Broad—making it the first restaurant in Memphis to specialize in Mexican-style food. Lake continued to operate the establishment until his retirement in 1955. His son Bill took over the operation but sold the company to Ilene Grohman, who ran the business until it closed in 1975.

In the 1920s, John E. Levy sold hot tamales at lunch stands across the city. Born in West Tennessee, Levy came to Memphis in the early 1900s and worked as a bread delivery driver when he was not gambling and drinking in local saloons. Later, Levy operated the Climax saloon at the corner of Monroe Avenue and Second Street, which the *Commercial Appeal* called a "chop suey parlor, hotel, and…gaming house." In 1917, Levy opened his first tamale stand at 56 South Fourth—his tamales were so popular that he soon built restaurants on Madison Avenue, Monroe Avenue, Third Street and Vance Avenue. By the early 1920s, Levy was a wealthy man and became known as the "Hot Tamale King of Memphis." This success afforded Levy plenty of time and money to pursue his love of gambling. According to his son, Erskine, "[My father] pull out a wad of bills and bet on anything. If you said it was going to rain, he would bet you it wouldn't." The fact that he was known to carry large sums of money proved to be his undoing.

On the evening of November 21, 1927, Levy left his home to gamble at the Antlers Poolroom on South Main Street with his friend Sam Gerstel. While he was there, Levy collected $600 from bets he had made on high school football games the weekend before. Around 11:00 p.m., Levy left the poolroom, and after dropping Gerstel at the Hotel Claridge, he returned to his home at 70 North Evergreen. While he was pulling into his three-car garage, Levy had just opened his car door when he was set upon by two masked men demanding money. Levy threw his wad of cash into the garage, and in retaliation, the bandits shot him in the chest with a .25 caliber handgun. "Son, they've killed me," Levy screamed when Erskine arrived on the scene. After being transported to Methodist Hospital, Levy was pronounced dead on arrival. The murder investigation was given to the city's first Jewish police detective, Morris Solomon, who used a gray felt hat left at the scene to find the killers. John Edwin Grace, Freeman T. Gunion and George W. Prince were found guilty and sentenced to death in 1930. Erskine continued to operate his father's lunch stands until he sold them sometime in the 1930s.

As we have seen, African Americans created the Mid-South version of the Mexican staple—what Chauncey Harley, owner of Hattie's Tamales, described as "tamales with soul." In the 1940s, Lester Dodson sold tamales out of his South Memphis home, on horseback and with a pushcart before launching fourteen tamale wagons in 1945. When a local grocery chain asked to stock his tamales, Dodson moved his operation to a commercial building. In a 1976 interview, Dodson explained how he named his business. "I told the phone company I was putting in a business and asked them if they had any names I could use. They [asked] what kind of business [it was]. I told 'em it was hot tamales. They said they had two names that sounded Spanish. I chose El Ranchito because it was the easiest name they had." Dodson's hot tamale enterprise flourished until the mid-1960s, when the health department began citing El Ranchito wagons for health violations.

Unwilling to abandon his business, Dodson designed a rolling cart that was acceptable to health inspectors. However, they required carts to stay in one place rather than roll about the city so that they could easily be inspected. This suited hot tamale peddler Robert Crawford, who kept his cart at the Lucky Food Store located at the corner of Park Avenue and Grand Street in the African American neighborhood of Orange Mound. Crawford's tamales cost twenty-five cents apiece and three dollars for a dozen. According to Crawford, it was not uncommon to sell over seven hundred hot tamales on a Saturday night. "There's two liquor stores at this intersection, and that helps the tamale business. They get a bottle at the liquor store and then they get some tamales from me. Then they're ready for anything.…The people you meet here are nice, friendly people. We're all one big, happy family. If there's trouble, we join hands and dodge bullets together," Crawford explained to *Commercial Appeal* reporter William Thomas in 1976. Dodson retired and closed El Ranchito in the late 1970s and passed away in 1987, but he is still remembered as the father of the hot tamale business in Memphis.

SHANGHAI CAFÉ

Perhaps the first Chinese restaurant in Memphis was the Oriental Café, which was opened in 1919 by Lau C. Chu at 342 Beale Street. In 1921, Lau C. Chu sold the business to Moy Ming, who changed the name to the Chop Suey Café. Chinese food was so popular among the easy riders of Beale Street that the 342 Beale location remained an Asian restaurant until the 1960s.

One of the most important Chinese restaurant owners was a young Cantonese farm laborer named Wong Kop, who made his way from famine-ridden China to the United States in 1907. Settling in Memphis in 1922, Wong operated several Chinese restaurants and became the recognized leader of the Bluff City's Chinese community. One of Wong's most popular restaurants was the Shanghai Café, located at 160–162 Hernando Street near Beale Street. Specializing in chop suey, Wong's café became very popular with non-Chinese Memphians looking for a cheap, hot meal after a night on the town. Later, he opened the Mandarin Inn on Union Avenue and became involved in civic affairs.

In the 1930s and 1940s, Harry Pang operated the Oriental Restaurant on North Third, while noted chef Lam Soon took over the operation of Wong's Mandarin Inn. Lee Yett moved to Memphis from Chicago and opened the Golden Pheasant Café with his partner, Sam Eng, at 166 Union Avenue at Third Street. "Memphis wanted and needed a first class Chinese restaurant," commented Lee. First class not only meant that the food was good but that the atmosphere was just right as well. When customers walked through the door, they found that the establishment was decked out in a red and gold color scheme and furniture decorated with the Chinese symbol for pheasant. Chef Jhan Eng specialized in both Chinese and American cuisine. "That has been the trouble with the ordinary Chinese restaurant, they couldn't cook American Food," explained Lee. To correct this, the Golden Pheasant served steaks, chops and seafood dishes in addition to chop suey and chow mein.

PETE AND JOE'S

Italians made their way to Memphis shortly before the Civil War. In 1850, there were thirty-two Italians living in Memphis, and twenty-one of them worked in coffeehouses; the rest were confectioners, bar-keepers and merchants, and one was a stonecutter. In the 1870s, the Italian population in Memphis swelled with the opening of vegetable farms that later became produce companies. As previously discussed, ravioli and spaghetti were available in some local eating establishments, but the first restaurant with a complete Italian menu was, allegedly, Pete and Joe's Place, which was opened in 1919 at 153 North Second Street and Washington Avenue, across from the Shelby County Courthouse.

Joe Locardi and his brother Pete—natives of Bassignana, Italy—opened their restaurant after Joe had spent several years managing dining rooms in Colorado, Chicago and St. Louis. Their sister, Julia Andreini, soon joined them, and according to the *Press-Scimitar* newspaper, "It [was] due greatly to her expert knowledge of Italian cookery that the place [was] able to achieve a reputation for choice Italian foods that [was] the envy of cafés and customers all over the country." On any given day, you could find the mayor of Memphis having lunch alongside other politicians, while doctors and lawyers savored Julia's spaghetti nearby.

In 1937, Pete and Joe took an extended trip to Italy while Julia ran the restaurant. One day, Julia received word that her brother Joe had died suddenly while staying in their hometown of Bassignana. When Pete decided to remain in Italy, Julia continued to operate the establishment until her own death two years later. When she died, the *Press-Scimitar* explained, "With the death of Mrs. Julia Andreini…will go much of the spirit of the little restaurant—whose spaghetti and spinach, the Italian way, brought to its tables the wealthy and the poor from coast to coast and many foreign countries." Julia's daughter Theresa took over the restaurant, which she operated with her husband, Joe Cortese Jr., until the late 1940s.

THE SOMBRERO

Although tamales became popular in Memphis in the 1920s, it was not until Frank and Maude Linche opened the Sombrero at 2693 Lamar Avenue in 1936 that a real Mexican restaurant was located in the Bluff City. The Linches operated the restaurant until 1946, when they sold it to Gene and Carolyn Lawson, who moved it to 4003 Lamar Avenue in 1961. The Sombrero was especially popular with visitors to Memphis who already loved Mexican food, including the star of the *Cisco Kid* television series, Duncan Renaldo. By the beginning of the 1970s, the Sombrero faced increased competition from the Memphis-based Pancho's restaurants, which opened a location on Bellevue in 1959, and the El Chico Mexican restaurant chain. As a result, Lawson closed the Sombrero in May 1973.

ONE MINUTE DAIRY LUNCH

The restaurant industry remained strictly segregated in Memphis—consequently, African Americans were not welcome at Britling's, Toddle House, Pete and Joe's or the Sombrero. So, African American entrepreneurs continued to operate restaurants exclusively for black Memphians. For example, Jimmy Bikas opened the One Minute Dairy Lunch in 1921 at 326 Beale Street. The One Minute specialized in pork sandwiches, hot dogs, chili dogs and root beer, and it was one of the most popular places on Beale Street. During the 1930s, the restaurant sold 3,600 hot dogs per day. In May

Bessie's Chicken Shack was one of the most popular African American restaurants in Memphis during the 1940s. *Courtesy of the Memphis and Shelby County Room, Memphis Public Libraries.*

1934, syndicated newspaper columnist Westbrook Pegler visited Memphis to cover the city's annual Cotton Carnival celebration. During his stay, he hitched a ride with a police detective who took him to Beale Street. While there, he visited the One Minute, where he witnessed a Memphian order a "snoot sandwich." Pegler turned to his companion and asked, "What did he say?" "He wants a pig-snoot sandwich," the detective sergeant said. "Very delicious eating, they say. A slice of pig-snoot fried in grease for a nickel. Or an order of pigtails, three on a plate, for a nickel or a dime. Or a fried hog's ear for a nickel."

Farther down Beale, at Fourth Street, was the Midway Café, which was opened in 1928. The restaurant served simple plate dinners, such as spaghetti and meatballs, but it was also known for its musical performances. According to historian Richard M. Raichelson, the "legendary café was well-known for its blues pianists.…In the back was a gambling room containing crap tables and next to it a room with a piano." Several famous blues piano players performed at the Midway, including Memphis Slim, Piano Red and Roosevelt Sykes.

By 1941, other restaurants owned by African Americans included the Black Cat Cafe at 202 Mulberry Street, the North Pole Sandwich Shop, the Home Café, Lone Star Eat Shop, Talk-O-Town, Eater's Place and the Harlem Café on Beale Street, the New Monte Carlo, located at 3168 Chelsea and the Servistan Grill, owned by Eva Russell, at 1019 Mississippi Avenue. Two of the most popular African American–owned restaurants were Bob's Steak Shop on Third Street, where they offered "the most choice steaks… chicken any style, sandwiches and 'the coldest beer in town,'" and Bessie's Chicken Shack, owned and operated by Bessie Toliver Harris. Located at 338 Vance Avenue, Bessie's Chicken Shack was built by Lonnie Harris, and he gave it to his wife to run. According to the Memphis Negro Chamber of

Commerce, "only the best foods [were] served at Bessie's Chicken Shack, only the best cooks [were] hired to cook the food; and only the best waitresses [were] permitted to serve this food."

THE STABLE

When America entered World War II, several war-related industries and military installations were located in Memphis—swelling the city's population and increasing the demand for food. Long hours and the rationing of certain foods made it easier for war-industry workers to eat in restaurants rather than try to cook at home. At the same time, soldiers and sailors on leave wanted to escape military chow and eat good food in local restaurants. To meet this demand, over 620 eating establishments were opened in Memphis during the conflict, and many of them operated on a twenty-four-hour-a-day basis. In the fall of 1942, diners were often unable to find a seat—the *Press-Scimitar* did a quick survey of 29 restaurants and found that in "6 of the 29 places, customers were standing and waiting for places to sit. Eleven others were full, with no vacant seats. Six had only a few available seats. Three had several places to sit and three were only half filled."

Soldiers were particularly fond of the Stable, located at 60 South Bellevue Boulevard. Opened in 1941 by George G. Early and Allen Gary, the restaurant took its name from a horse barn that once occupied the site. The Stable specialized in a four-ounce filet mignon served with mushrooms as well as shrimp and lobster thermidor. According to *Commercial Appeal* reporter Lloyd Dinkins, Chef H. Albert Waller "[didn't] flinch when four of his regular customers [would come] in and start with 18 shrimp on ice, consume a main course of 10 fried shrimp and let down easily with the five-shrimp platter." The Stable remained a popular eating destination well after the war ended. In October 1960, the Stable closed to make way for the construction of the Admiral Benbow Inn, a 134-unit motel. "It kinda breaks my heart," Waller said.

IN THE 1940s, MORE AND more restaurants in Memphis also began to specialize in barbecued pork. In the 1945 Memphis City Directory, one local restaurant proclaimed: "Leonard's Pit Barbecue Is Supreme. As Memphis Knows So Will America." In the years after World War II, barbecue became Memphis's signature food—it was known throughout the nation, just as Leonard's predicted.

3

"Struttin' with Some Barbecue"

As sandwich shops sprang up in and around Memphis in the 1920s, many of them offered pork sandwiches along with hamburgers and hot dogs. Barbecued pork is believed to have first appeared when Spanish explorer Hernando de Soto brought a small herd of pigs with him to North America in 1539. According to Memphis barbecue historian Craig David Meek, "De Soto and his troops passed through present-day South Carolina, where the newly introduced pigs met the traditional Native American practice of cooking meat with smoke and indirect heat to create what today's southerners recognize as barbecue." Smoked pork sandwiches and pulled pork could be found at many lunch stands and cafés throughout the city, especially on Beale Street. Barbecue's growing popularity in the early decades of the twentieth century was reflected in two musical compositions written by Memphians. In W.C. Handy's "Beale Street Blues," the famous blues composer mentioned "hog-nose restaurants," and jazz composer and pianist Lil Hardin Armstrong titled one of her masterpieces "Struttin' with Some Barbecue."

LEONARD'S PIT BARBECUE

Born in 1896, Leonard Heuberger was the son of German immigrants who lived on South Third Street with his Italian and Irish neighbors. After graduating from Christian Brothers School, Heuberger joined the navy, where

(Continued on page 29)

As Memphis Knows, So Will America OUR PIT BARBECUE IS SUPREME!

Serving Real . . .
PIT BARBECUE

The Barbecue Bean Pot

The Half and Half Plate
(½ Spaghetti and
½ Barbecue)

Custom Barbecuing For
Picnics and Parties

LEONARD'S PIT BARBECUE
Mr Brown — Miss White

We Serve . . .

Breakfast, Lunch
and Dinner

IN MEMPHIS
FOR 44 YEARS

McLEMORE at BELLEVUE   Open 7 a.m. - 2 a.m.

Page 28

Leonard Heuberger invented Memphis-style barbecue with his pulled pork and coleslaw sandwich. *Courtesy of the Memphis and Shelby County Room, Memphis Public Libraries.*

he served as paymaster for the USS *Yale* during World War I. Looking back on his military career, Heuberger later remembered that he crossed the English Channel ninety-eight times during the war. When he returned to Memphis, Heuberger went to work as a salesman for the Cudahy Packing company until 1922, when he traded a Ford Model T for a small hamburger stand located at the South Memphis intersection of Trigg Avenue and Latham Street. Heuberger renamed the stand to Leonard's Lunchroom, and it offered barbecue along with hamburgers and soft drinks. One day, an African American woman from the nearby neighborhood walked up to the stand and shared with him her secret barbecue sauce. When Heuberger added her sauce and coleslaw to his pulled pork sandwich, he invented Memphis-style barbecue. The ingredients of Heuberger's sandwich soon spread across Memphis, and over time, it became the city's signature culinary dish. Leonard's pulled pork sandwich also was the first of several innovations that secured Memphis's place as the barbecue capital of the world.

Heuberger purchased land at the corner of Bellevue Boulevard and McLemore Avenue in 1932 and built Leonard's Pit Barbecue, one of the first Memphis restaurants to offer a pork-dominated menu. When Heuberger counted the money in his register on the restaurant's opening day, he was disappointed to learn that he had made only $7.50. The situation did not get any better when Heuberger made a misstep that almost cost him his business. It has previously been stated that 1931 and 1932 were the worst years of the Depression, during which many cafés and lunchrooms failed and shuttered their doors. Despite the economic downturn, Heuberger decided to raise the price of his sandwich from ten to fifteen cents. Many customers were unable to afford the new price, and they knew that they could grab a five-cent hamburger at a nearby Owl Lunchroom. When customers stopped coming, Leonard's started offering two sandwiches for a quarter, and business quickly rebounded. According to Richard H. Jacobs, who later became president of the company, "People who didn't even know each other would get acquainted on the spot and split the cost of a couple of sandwiches." Then, Heuberger got lucky. Bellevue Boulevard was designated as the main corridor to lead travelers into and out of Mississippi, and as a result, Leonard's became a designated stop for a regional bus line. Soon after, the State of Tennessee extended Highway 51 to Bellevue Boulevard, which increased traffic and business even more.

On July 4, 1938, Heuberger hired fourteen-year-old James Willis to stack and clean trays for seventy cents a day. When business was slow, Willis watched as the pitmaster, Tom Tillman, slowly cooked barbecue. Willis said, "[I] learned everything from him.…[He] showed me how to trim it. Showed me when to turn it. When to make a fire. Tell when I did a batch of tough meat, tell me what I did wrong." Willis was promoted to cook in 1940 and worked at Leonard's well into the twenty-first century. In 2002, the Southern Foodways Alliance interviewed Willis for its Memphis, Tennessee BBQ Project. During the course of the interview, Willis described how barbecue cooking changed over his fifty-year-long career:

> *Well, you had to have somebody put it on. Keep a fire under it. Turn it every hour and a half, two hours and know when to put out the fire. See…they got it now where they puts it in these pits and then turn it to 250–350–180* [degrees], *whatever they want it on, and it stays there. Nobody have to turn it. Nobody have to look at it. Nothing. When that times up, it's done.*

The Southern Foodways Alliance said of Willis: "[He is] an archetypal Southern pitmaster. He has, for the great majority of his career, worked in obscurity, tending the pits day and night, cooking the best pork barbecue he can." The organization also honored him with its Ruth Fertel Keeper of the Flame Award in 2002.

As previously discussed, Heuberger learned a lot about barbecue sauce from his African American neighbors. He also grew up with Italian Memphians, so he almost certainly was familiar with Italian forms of cooking. At some point, Hueberger added spaghetti as a side dish on Leonard's menu. Like the pulled pork sandwich, Heuberger mixed these two traditional dishes together to create the half-barbecue, half-spaghetti plate—an innovation that further cemented Memphis's place as an important barbecue center. In 1952, for example, Leonard's prepared ten thousand pulled pork sandwiches for a picnic celebrating the twenty-fifth anniversary of the Bruce Lumber Company.

Since its inception, Leonard's offered drive-in service. James Willis recalled his days as a carhop: "You could see a car, I'd say, a half a block away, and

Scrappers enjoyed meeting at **Leonard's** after a big game, a special occasion, or a casual date.

THERE'S A BARBEQUE SIGN ON EVERY CORNER, BUT ONLY ONE

LEONARD'S

Serving Real Pit Barbeque . . . Hot Off the Pit

IN MEMPHIS OVER 39 YEARS

McLemore at Bellevue   948-1581

South Side High School students enjoying the barbecue at Leonard's. *Courtesy of the Memphis and Shelby County Room, Memphis Public Libraries.*

you know what he wanted before he come in the driveway. That car-hoppin'. they stopped there in the street down there at Bellevue and McLemore every Sunday evening from I'd say from about 4:30 'til about 6:30. That street would be stopped for them folks getting into that place." Drive-in service reached its zenith in the 1950s; at that time, Leonard's became a popular hangout for teenagers. On the weekends, the parking lot would be filled with high school students coming from basketball and football games, dances or just ending a night of cruising around. According to longtime customer Bill Russell, "Leonard's was the safe hang out. From the ages of seventeen to twenty-one, I spent many a Friday and Saturday night at Leonard's…having white pig sandwiches with chocolate milk. Back then, they had dark or white meat sandwiches. We always tried to park back by the smoker because it smelled so good."

Leonards was so popular in the 1950s that it served between six thousand and ten thousand pounds of barbecue per week. To meet this increased demand, Heuberger expanded his operation to include a new vestibule as well as additional parking and seating. In addition, Heuberger had tile-setter Wallace Collins embed thirty-five silver dollars in the restaurant's floor to acknowledge the number of years that he had been in business. During the weekend of November 24 and 25, 1956, Leonard's celebrated its thirty-fifth anniversary by hosting Miss Barbecue of 1956 and giving away barbecued pigs as door prizes. One of Leonard's most faithful guests was Elvis Presley, who, before his death in 1977, often ate there. According to longtime employee Dan Brown, "On some evenings, the restaurant would get a call right before closing saying Elvis wanted to come in after-hours with his friends. The group often stayed until sunrise."

Heuberger surprised many in August 1968 when he sold the restaurant to a group of investors led by T.W. "Bill" Hoehn Jr., president of Hoehn Chevrolet. The syndicate promised that Heuberger would remain in charge and that "no changes [were] contemplated." Hoehn was named president of the corporation with Richard Jacobs as vice president and Leon Ray as the secretary-treasurer. Despite the change in ownership, all of the longtime employees, who made Leonard's such a Memphis institution, remained—the cooks were Tom Tillman and his wife, Annie, the cook's assistant was Madie Lee, the sandwich maker was Jack Patterson, the pitmasters were James Willis and Milton Smith, the slaw chef was Ernestine Ford and the veteran car captains were Walter Polk, William Winfield and John Stephens. Other significant employees were Nina Ashbrenner, Rod Bernard, Bernice Clark, Eva Childress, Harry Clutts, Ruth Ellis, Mabel Lawrence, Margaret Lenti, Edith Overstreet, Frances Riffenberry, Ruth Rogers, Murline Snider and Heuberger's grandson, Tommy Hughes, and the managers were Bert Reed and Lonnie Hunt.

The new corporation provided Leonard's with enough capital to establish a franchise program and offer a catering service. A fleet of vans brought a full menu to customers, including not only barbecue sandwiches but also ribs, chicken, hamburgers, seafood, coleslaw and potato salad. By 1975, there were nine Leonard's franchises throughout Memphis, including locations on Madison Avenue, Second Street, Union Avenue, Park Avenue and Summer Avenue, which produced thirty-five thousand pork shoulders per year. In addition to catering and franchising, Leonard's also shipped barbecue across the country. In 1979, Richard Jacobs reported:

> *There's a doctor in Chicago, who has a house in Florida, that visits four or five times a year. On his flight home, he routes himself through Memphis and has us make fifty barbecue sandwiches at a time. He puts them in his freezer, then takes a sandwich to his office every day and heats it up in a microwave oven. His wife once told me that if her husband didn't have some barbecues in the freezer, he gets spastic.*

An air force general shipped Leonard's barbecue, beans and slaw to the Pentagon for a five-hundred-person event. A case of Leonard's barbecue sauce was shipped to a person in Denver every two months and a Carlsbad, California auto dealer purchased two pork shoulders every summer for picnics.

After forty-six years in the restaurant business, Leonard Heuberger, the father of Memphis-style barbecue, died after a short illness. Despite this loss, the business continued to flourish through the 1980s. Jacobs continued as president and Dan Brown—who had started at Leonard's as a sandwich maker when he was fifteen years old—was the general manager. The locations on Elvis Presley Boulevard and South Mendenhall remained popular, and in 1987, a new location opened at 5465 Fox Plaza Drive. However, as the 1990s began, the company decided to close the Bellevue location and move its main operation to Fox Plaza. Hundreds of Memphians poured into the old building to say goodbye. Cashier Bernice Clark, who worked at Leonard's for twenty-nine years, summed it up for many when she said, "This is breaking my heart. I hate to see the place go, not just for me but for Memphis—it's a landmark."

Dan Brown eventually bought the operation and continues to serve barbecue at the Fox Plaza location, but it's the Bellevue Restaurant that continues to be remembered by scores of mid-southerners. Memphian Janet Price recalled:

> When I was a young child, growing up, we lived in north Mississippi. On special occasions, or just for fun, we would all load up in the car and go to Leonard's Barbecue. This was in the late 1940s [and] early 1950s. It was and still is the best food I have ever eaten!…That pork was devine [sic] and the slaw—unbelievable!…What a thrill it was for me, as a kid, to go to the drive-in, have the gentleman put the tray on the car window and smell those fabulous smells!

BERRETTA'S

In the early 1920s, Louis Berretta Sr. sold produce to local grocery stores—including those owned by Clarence Saunders, the founder of the Piggly Wiggly and sole owner of My Name grocery store chains. Berretta's wife, Rosa Vescovi, explained: "I remember he used to discuss how he would take

Berretta's was a popular hangout for high school and college students in Memphis during the 1950s and 1960s. *Courtesy of the Memphis and Shelby County Room, Memphis Public Libraries.*

orders from all types of farm produce from the stores…and then buy them at the market on Beale and Front for resale to the stores." In 1927, he opened his own grocery at 1615 Union and later expanded to a second location far from midtown. Park Avenue was a narrow tar-capped road when the grocer purchased a service station and grocery store there in 1933. Located outside the city limits, it was surrounded by a few homes and cornfields. A mile or so down the gravel-lined road of Highland Avenue was a small business center that contained a movie theater, a billiard parlor, a drugstore, a Kroger, a Piggly Wiggly, a hardware store, a barbershop and the Sunnyside Inn Restaurant. A few blocks from the business center was the West Tennessee State Teacher's College (later renamed the University of Memphis).

Berretta's gas station and grocery store became a popular spot for those looking for a quick bite or a bottle of beer. Farmers carrying wagonloads of produce to Memphis often stopped there along with truck drivers heading to and from nearby Highway 78. As traffic in the area and the demand for food increased, Berretta built a barbecue pit and sold pork shoulder and Memphis's Goldcrest 51 beer to hungry and thirsty passersby. Berretta's son, Louis Jr., delivered barbecue sandwiches to the surrounding neighborhood, and when Kennedy Army Hospital opened in 1942 on nearby Getwell Road, business increased dramatically. At that time, much of the grocery store was converted into a lunchroom that contained a long counter, simple tables and chairs and a jukebox. Known then as the Famous Bar Beer Que Inn, they served barbecue sandwiches for twenty-five cents, hamburgers for fifteen cents and spiced ham sandwiches for thirty cents. "During the 1940s, our restaurant was publicized as selling more beer on premises than anyplace in town…we were running through two thousand cases a month," Louis Jr. explained.

In 1951, the name of the restaurant was changed to Berretta's Famous Bar-B-Q, and they added T-shaped carports for curb service. Louis Jr. remembered: "Memphis was the drive-in capital of the world back then. We had to hire a security guard to direct traffic, the same as Leonard's and a lot of other restaurants on the cruising circuit." For the Hollywood actress Stella Stevens, who grew up in a nearby neighborhood, Berretta's was her "favorite teen hangout." Another famous Memphis teenager also liked to frequent Berretta's: "Elvis used to come in when he was just getting popular. He'd walk straight through to the jukebox….He'd play some of his songs, then sit down and have a sandwich." Berretta's restaurant was not only popular with high school students but also with college students from the University of Memphis. According to Berretta's son, Louis Jr., "At night, after the library closed, they'd all come down here. They'd just fill the place up."

In addition to the security guard and six carhops, cooks Mattie Coleman and William K. Hall prepared the barbecue, spaghetti, pizza and other Italian entrées that were developed by Berretta's wife, Rosa. In addition to an expanded menu, the restaurant added a family dining room in 1956 to accommodate customers who wanted a more formal atmosphere. The founder of the restaurant, Louis Berretta Sr., passed away in 1968, and his son, Louis Jr., took control of the business. Around the time of the founder's death, the demand for drive-in service declined and was discontinued—but, overall, business remained strong through the 1970s and early 1980s. However, by the middle of the 1980s, the restaurant needed remodeling that would have cost thousands of dollars. Fearing he would not get enough of a return for such a large investment, Louis Jr. closed the restaurant in December 1985 and sold the property to a South Carolina developer, who built a convenience store, gas station and laundry at the location. The following year, Louis Jr. and his son, Louis III, opened Berretta's Spike and Rail Restaurant in the Memphis suburb of Bartlett, which they operated until 1997. Louis Berretta Jr. died in November 2007 after a lifetime in the restaurant industry.

PIG 'N WHISTLE

In 1929, an Atlanta-based restaurant chain called the Pig 'n Whistle opened a franchise at 1579 Union that offered sandwiches. Open from 6:00 a.m. to

Let Pig'n Whistle Help You Enjoy the
Carnival

Two Air-Conditioned Restaurants to Serve You

No. 1—1579 UNION   No. 2—21 SO. SECOND
(CURB SERVICE ALSO)

PIG'N WHISTLE OF MEMPHIS, Inc.
HERBERT HOOD, JR., *President*

Opened in 1929 on Union Avenue, the Pig 'n Whistle was a popular barbecue restaurant until it closed in 1966. *Courtesy of the Memphis and Shelby County Room, Memphis Public Libraries.*

3:00 a.m., the Pig 'n Whistle was designed like an old English cottage with a distinctive sign bearing a dancing pig that was blowing a whistle. In 1934, Herbert Hood Jr. bought the restaurant and formed the Pig 'n Whistle of Memphis Inc., a closed corporation. Hood expanded the menu and put an emphasis on barbecue and fried foods. Hood explained: "We…specialize in deep fried foods, because they are healthy and easily digested."

The dining room, known as the Pig Pen, was air-conditioned, and there was an outdoor beer garden called the Bier Terrasse. Sales quickly doubled, and the Pig, as it was affectionately called, became one of the city's most popular gathering places. As a teenager in the mid-1940s, newspaper columnist John Knott loved to hang out there: "The Pig had a huge parking lot and a small inside place that seemed always to be jammed with everyone talking at the top of his voice. Beer flowed freely and the jukebox was deafening." For Louis Fineberg, the restaurant "was like going to heaven." He said, "You'd spend your whole weekend there."

Like Leonard's and Berretta's, the Pig offered curb service. This service was provided by dedicated carhops like T.J. Murray, who was nicknamed "Flops" for being as quick as a rabbit. James "Preacher" Gordon was the head carhop, and many influential Memphians, such as Coca-Cola bottler Everett Pidgeon, insisted on being served by him. In 1945, Hood sold his shares, and Louise Cramer became the majority stockholder and president of the company. Cramer changed the focus of the restaurant from a barbecue shop and teenage hangout to a dining room for adults. This change was successful during the 1950s, but, by the middle of the next decade, the Pig's customer base began to dwindle. The business was also in need of $100,000 worth of remodeling, which Cramer felt the company could not afford. As a result, the Pig 'n Whistle closed on October 2, 1966. "To me, it brings a lump, a feeling hard to explain. Probably sometime, I'll be sitting across the street just looking at the place," sighed Preacher Gordon.

THE BARBECUE KINGS OF BEALE STREET

Just off Beale Street, there were two barbecue restaurants that served both African American and white diners. Walter Culpepper opened Culpepper's Chicken Shack in 1936 with his wife, Hattie. Located on Fourth Street, the restaurant became a popular destination for worn-out gamblers, musicians and sex workers who finished their evenings munching on Culpepper's food. Although the restaurant was called the Chicken Shack, it was Culpepper's barbecue that drew most of his clientele. Two years after opening, a fire destroyed the Fourth Street location, so Culpepper moved to Beale and Hernando, where his business increased dramatically.

According to Culpepper's niece, Freddie L. Moore: "When people went out on the town and had a good time, the evening wasn't over until you went to the Chicken Shack. You never knew who you'd see there—celebrities and people in tuxedos standing next to folks in jeans." Two of those celebrities were disc jockey Dewey Phillips and Sun Records owner Sam Phillips (no relation), who are both considered to be founders of rock 'n' roll. Dewey was an icon on Beale, and he was beloved by the African American community. When he would finish recording his show, *Red, Hot and Blue* on WHBQ radio, he would often stop by Culpepper's for a plate of barbecue with Sam in tow. The singer that both men discovered, Elvis Presley, also frequented Culpepper's. Always a polite man, Elvis called the owner "Mr. Culpepper," which was disconcerting to some of his fellow white southerners. When asked why he called him Mr. Culpepper, Elvis replied, "I've been calling him Mister all along, why would I change now?"

Culpepper was one of the most beloved people in the Beale Street area. He and his wife had no children, but they doted on the neighborhood's kids, who could count on a free meal and help with school and finding a job. In his later years, Culpepper was in the hospital when the attending physician said, "I know you, Mr. Culpepper. I was one of your alley kids you used to feed." Walter and Hattie continued to run the Chicken Shack until 1971. Hattie died in 1992, and Mr. Culpepper passed in 1995.

Johnny Mills operated his own restaurant at Fourth and Beale, where he declared himself the barbecue king of Memphis, and many agreed with him. When he wasn't at the Chicken Shack with Dewey, Sam Phillips was yearning for Johnny Mills's barbecue. In a 1992 interview, Sam remembered:

> [I could smell] *Johnny Mills's barbecue from on top of the Peabody, while I was putting the bands out on CBS in the Plantation Room. Johnny Mills…cooking that barbecue like you have never smelled in your life. You couldn't get too mad or too drunk not to smell Johnny Mills barbecue, even when the wind was blowing in the other direction.*

The aroma of pulled pork that Phillips described wafted throughout much of downtown, because Mills prepared his barbecue in an open pit located in an alley behind his restaurant. Singer Bing Crosby, whose first wife, Dixie Lee, was from Memphis, also loved to eat at Johnny Mills. Whenever he passed through the city, he made a point of stopping at Fourth and Beale. Many white Memphians felt comfortable at Johnny Mills because there were two dining rooms—one for white customers and the other for African American customers.

TOPS

In 1952, J.W. Lawson opened a small barbecue sandwich shop at 3382 Macon Road, near National, that he called Tops. Using charcoal and green hickory wood, Lawson cooked whole shoulders for ten hours, from which he made his popular jumbo barbecue sandwich that he served with a side of beans. Tops soon expanded; in 1960, Lawson had restaurants on Jackson Avenue, Park Avenue, Rhodes Avenue, near Getwell Road, and Thomas Street. In 1964, Granville E. "George" Messick went to work for Lawson and oversaw all of the stores as general manager. Messick and Lawson took a very conservative approach to building their restaurant chain—they expanded only when the market justified opening another location. By 1970, the operation had grown to ten restaurants spread across the city.

Besides their conservative approach to expansion, another key element of Tops's success was in training master cooks to oversee the preparation of the pork shoulders. Pat Mann, who started working at Tops in 1969, trained the master cooks well into the twenty-first century. "Great barbecue begins with a good fire—hickory wood to add flavor and hot coals that are spread evenly. The pork shoulders should be placed about two inches apart on the grill, and they should be turned after six hours of slow grilling," explained Mann.

Lawson retired in 1984, and Messick bought the business with George "Monte" Montague, who served as the general manager. In a 2002 interview with the Southern Foodways Alliance, Montague explained Tops's commitment to cooking pork "the old-fashioned way": "I know a lot of the people that are in the barbecue business now have gone to these stainless steel cookers, and they have timers and all of the conveniences, but they are not able to turn out the type of barbecue that we do." When Messick died in 2016, his wife, Eugenia Lauderdale Messick, and Montague promised their "more than 150 employees that Tops Bar-B- Q [would] continue with quality and service to uphold its legacy as the oldest and only independent barbecue chain in the Mid-South." Tops continues to serve over thirty thousand barbecue sandwiches per week at its fifteen locations in Memphis and Marion, Arkansas, and Olive Branch and Southaven, Mississippi.

BRADY AND LIL'S

At 601 South Parkway East, Brady Vincent and his wife, Lillie, opened a small restaurant called Brady and Lil's. Vincent had been a railroad cook who liked nothing better than to experiment with food. When he opened his restaurant, he played around with different meats until he settled on Boston butts rather than pork shoulder to make his barbecue. Vincent also invented barbecue spaghetti, which was described by longtime customer Troy Henderson as "so good it was sinful." By marinating the meat before cooking, Brady and Lil's was able to give the slow-cooked meat a tender quality that other Memphis barbecue restaurants did not have. Brady and Lil's was frequented by local musicians from nearby Royal Studios and Stax Records—legendary band leader and producer Willie Mitchell loved Brady's barbecue. Another of Brady's loyal customers was Frank Vernon, who lived in the area and managed a restaurant.

In 1980, Brady told Vernon that he was planning to retire and asked if he'd like to buy the business. Vernon quickly agreed, and once the papers were signed, he took a crash course from Vincent on how to cook barbecue. Within a few years, Vernon opened a second Brady and Lil's at Knight Arnold and Mendenhall Roads, but it became apparent to him and his son, Eric, that they had expanded too fast. As Eric Vernon remembered: "We felt like we moved too far from our original crowd. We decided to look for somewhere in Midtown, where we would be between South Memphis and

East Memphis." They chose to settle at 1782 Madison, which was renamed the Bar-B-Q Shop in November 1987.

THREE LITTLE PIGS OF AMERICA

In the early 1960s, McDonald's hamburgers and other fast food franchises were slowly beginning to appear across the United States. Many restaurant owners followed the fast food model very closely in hopes of replicating their success. One such restaurateur was Frank O. Howell Jr., the owner of the Little Pigs barbecue shops at 671 South Highland Street, 548 East Mallory Avenue, 620 Semmes Street and 2150 Young Avenue. In October 1960, he was approached by sales executive Ben F. Burch and his business partner and life insurance sales manager, Bill N. Newman, with the idea of franchising his Little Pigs operation. Howell was receptive, and the three formed the Three Little Pigs of America in January 1962.

The concept of fast food barbecue sandwiches appealed to businessmen in many parts of the country. For example, Glenn Ledebur of Beverly Hills, California, was contracted to open sixty-eight restaurants in the Los Angeles area, and Ed Sloper bought franchises for twenty units in Chicago. "I've seen some wonderful business opportunities, but this is more exciting than any of

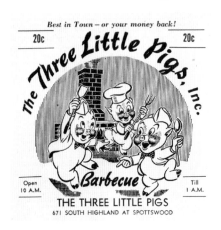

Before it went bankrupt, Three Little Pigs franchised barbecue sandwich shops all across the United States. *Courtesy of the Memphis and Shelby County Room, Memphis Public Libraries.*

them," Ledebur said. By July 1962, the Three Little Pigs of America had sold 379 franchises in 24 states, and they hoped to sell 2,500 units in the United States and Canada. The company never lacked for ambition— in 1965, the company laid plans to open restaurants in Europe. "Our aim is to replace the European favorite, croissant, with a barbecue sandwich," said one company executive.

Unfortunately, the national chain grew too fast, and consumer demand did not meet expectations, forcing the company to declare bankruptcy in 1967. Meanwhile, the original Highland location continued to serve barbecue well into the twenty-first century. In 1981, the location was bought by a Wisconsin transplant named Beverly Musarra, who ran the restaurant with her husband, Dominic, and their seven children until July 2003.

LOEB'S TENNESSEE PIT

In the late 1950s, A.B. Coleman and his colleague, Porter Moss, were tired of working at the Fred Montesi grocery store on Summer Avenue. Across the street sat a Tops restaurant, and both men eventually went to work for the barbecue chain. Coleman didn't stay at Tops for long; in 1962, he left to start his own restaurant, which he planned to call Tasty Bar-B-Q. Looking for a suitable location, Coleman approached William Loeb, the secretary-treasurer of his family's laundry business, to rent a piece of property for his first restaurant. "I didn't know anything about barbecue when Mr. Coleman walked into the office to ask about renting a building we owned for a stand, but he intrigued me, and I began to learn," Loeb explained.

The laundry executive partnered with Coleman and businessman Jack Scharff to form the Amelia Company, which established a Loeb's Tasty Bar-B-Q at 3178 Summer Avenue, five blocks west of Highland Street, in 1963. Seventeen months later, there were eighteen Loeb's barbecue restaurants in Memphis, including one at 1055 South Bellevue Boulevard, which was advertised as the largest barbeque sandwich shop in the nation. The restaurant had two large pits that had the capacity to cook a ton of pulled pork every day, and there was seating available for eighty customers. As Loeb explained: "We are considering going into other states with our operation, and the newest shop will help us determine whether there should be many small shops in a city or several large ones." As this quote suggests, the dream of creating a national barbecue chain captured Loeb's imagination, as well as several others'.

The name of the restaurant chain was changed to Loeb's Tennessee Pit Bar-B-Q in 1965, when the number of shops increased to twenty-two locations and plans were laid to add many more. "We are doing it the careful way. We own sixteen of the twenty-two buildings and we have been slow to award franchises. We could have sold about one hundred franchises at $4,000 each, but we waited until we had the staff to supervise them thoroughly," Loeb stated in April 1965. The company reported that they were selling four tons of barbecue per day, which was smoked for twelve hours while sauce that was prepared at their commissary was delivered to each restaurant by a fleet of twelve trucks.

William Loeb collaborated with singer Pat Boone to franchise Loeb's Tennessee Pit Bar-B-Q restaurants, like this one located at the corner of Summer Avenue and White Station Road. *Courtesy of the Memphis and Shelby County Room, Memphis Public Libraries.*

Two months later, in June 1965, Loeb formed the LoBo Corporation with singer Pat Boone to franchise the barbeque shops across the nation. At the time, Loeb's Tennessee Pit Bar-B-Q claimed to be "the South's largest home-owned Bar-B-Q chain," and, by early 1966, there were twenty-four shops in Memphis, two in Arkansas, eight in Mississippi and one in Alabama. Despite these successes, there was a major problem growing within the company—Loeb and his general manager, A.B. Coleman, could not get along. So, Loeb bought out the contracts of Coleman and Vice President Porter Moss to reorganize the company in January 1966. Moss, who would go on to own and operate several Showboat Barbecue restaurants, stated that Coleman and Loeb were "too busy trying to screw each other over" to concentrate on growing the business properly.

The former general manager then opened his own Coleman's Bar-B-Q restaurants in the Memphis area. Like his former employer, Coleman's grew quickly—by the early 1970s, there were ten Coleman's Bar-B-Q restaurants in the Memphis area. William Loeb, however, soon had his revenge. He reported to the Internal Revenue Service that Coleman had used company funds for his personal income, which he did not report on his tax return. After being indicted on two counts of tax fraud, Coleman argued at his April 1972 trial that he was forced to take company funds because Loeb was cutting into his profit sharing by charging personal debt to the company. Coleman was found guilty of tax evasion and given a suspended sentence.

The feud and indictment drained both companies—Coleman's soon went out of business, while Loeb's continued to operate barbecue restaurants into the 1980s. There was another reason Loeb's Tennessee Pit Bar-B-Q ultimately failed; in 1968, Loeb's brother, Henry, became the mayor of Memphis. Just one month after Henry's election, African American sanitation workers went on strike, which led to the murder of famed civil rights leader Dr. Martin Luther King Jr. During the strike, Loeb-owned businesses, including the barbecue shops, were targeted by vandals and boycotted by strike supporters. Even after the strike was finally settled following Dr. King's death, many Memphians refused to buy anything with the name Loeb on it.

THE RENDEZVOUS

Charlie Vergos grew up in the restaurant world. His father, John C. Vergos, was a Greek immigrant who owned a café called Joe's Place at Second and Beale Streets. His father's café specialized in hot dogs and chili made with Greek spices. After serving as a combat infantryman in Europe during World War II, Charlie Vergos returned to Memphis and opened Wimpy's, a tavern and sandwich shop located in the alley known as November Sixth Street, in 1948. Selling beer and ham and cheese sandwiches, Wimpy's did not attract enough customers, and Vergos was forced to close the tavern in the early 1950s. According to the *1955 Memphis City Directory*, Vergos worked as a waiter at the Coney Island Café owned by John G. Touliatos. Three years later, he was working at David and Hattie Byler's Rendevous Café located at 2021 Madison Avenue. In 1964, he left the Bylers and opened the Uptown Rendevous in the basement of 66 South November Sixth Street, between Main and Second Streets. As he did at Wimpy's, Vergos specialized in ham and cheese sandwiches, and his new restaurant became a popular hangout for men who were waiting while their wives shopped in downtown stores.

The restaurant's meat supplier, Louis Feinberg, suggested to Vergos that he needed to expand his menu. "I know that," Charlie responded, "but I don't know what to do." Feinberg tried to offer baked chickens, but Vergos's customers had no interest in eating them. Feinberg then offered pork ribs, but Vergos was reluctant to cook them. "I don't know very much about ribs," Vergos replied. Fortunately for him, he had an employee who did. Little John (his last name has been lost to history, but his contribution has not) knew how to cook ribs using vinegar, "because it [made] them tender and it [helped] keep

famous for . . .
charcoal broiled ribs
ham and cheese sandwiches
michelob on draft
November 6th St. (The Alley)
at Union between Main and 2nd.

Charlie Vergos Rendezvous

DINERS CLUB CARDS HONORED

©Hertz System, Inc., 1967

Charlie Vergos opened his iconic barbecue ribs restaurant, the Rendezvous, in 1968. *Courtesy of the Memphis and Shelby County Room, Memphis Public Libraries.*

the fire down a bit," he explained. Vergos then created a dry rub for the ribs, which included the Greek spices his father used in his chili. Known as dry ribs, Vergos's creation revolutionized the barbecue industry, just as Leonard Hueberger's and Brady Vincent's creations had.

Food Network chef David Rosengarten described Vergos as the "king" who created "the best ribs you'll ever taste in your life." In 1968, Vergos moved the Rendezvous to the basement of 52 South Second, directly across from the Peabody Hotel. Downtown Memphis in 1968 was not an auspicious location to expand a business—even a well-regarded one. Memphians and visitors alike abandoned downtown, but Vergos refused to budge. He was committed to Memphis and became a leader in revitalization efforts to save the downtown area. As his son, John, recalled: "One reason my father was so civic-minded was that he was always grateful to the citizens of Memphis who supported the business." Echoing this sentiment, Memphis mayor A.C. Wharton called Vergos an "icon for saving Downtown." The Rendezvous was not only beloved by Memphians but also by the city's many tourists. Presidents Bill Clinton and George W. Bush ate there, as well as Mick Jagger and the British princes, William and Harry. Charlie Vergos died in March 2010, but his restaurant continues to serve its signature dry ribs to this day.

GRIDLEY'S

Clyde Gridley was working as an accounting comptroller for Loeb's when he decided to open his own barbecue business. However, he wanted his restaurant to be different. Instead of the fast food atmosphere of Loeb's or the working-class flavor of Berretta's and Leonard's, Gridley brought a sense of fine dining to the pulled pork world when he opened Gridley's

Fine Bar-B-Q on Summer Avenue near Graham Street in 1975. He hired waiters from the old Peabody Hotel and had them wear tuxedoes with bow ties and white gloves and carry white towels on their arms. Gridley's specialized in ribs, and Gridley himself was so meticulous in his preparation that he designed a unique knife to butcher the carcasses in such a way that more meat was left on the bones. Four years after opening his first restaurant, Gridley opened a second location on Macon Road. In 1981, the two stores took in $5.8 million in gross revenue, and, in 1982, the restaurants sold twelve thousand pounds of ribs and eighteen thousand pounds of pork shoulder per week.

Like Little Pigs and his former employer, Loeb's, Gridley wanted to create a national barbecue chain. His first franchise opened in Jackson, Mississippi, in September 1982, and he had contracts out for franchises in Nashville, Tennessee, and Omaha, Nebraska when disaster struck. After a long day at the original location, Gridley was driving down Summer Avenue, just after midnight on December 12, 1983, when he suffered a heart attack. His vehicle swerved across the center line, striking another car head-on. The driver and passenger in the other vehicle were not hurt, but Gridley was pronounced dead when he was taken to Methodist North Hospital.

Following Gridley's death, two more Memphis locations were opened, but his dream of a national barbecue chain died with him. Gridley's wife, Celeste, and his daughters, Robyn Nickell and Vickie Henry, continued running the operation. In 1986, they began bottling and selling their barbecue sauce in area grocery stores and hoped to make it a nationwide product. Unfortunately, the company went bankrupt at the end of the 1980s, and while a group of investors attempted to continue the business, it never achieved the success it reached in the early 1980s.

THE PUBLIC EYE AND CORKY'S

In late 1972, Bailey Weiner renovated his property on the west side of Cooper Avenue in the Overton Square entertainment district. The location had previously included a barbershop, an office supply store and the Hi Hat Café before Weiner gutted the building to make space for a new barbecue restaurant owned by East High School graduate Dick Fisher. Named the Public Eye, the restaurant initially offered a simple menu of barbecue ribs, baked ham and charbroiled chicken served with baked beans, slaw and

French bread. Over time, however, the restaurant added a barbecue plate and sandwich, barbecue chicken, steak, roast beef and salads.

When the Public Eye opened on February 16, 1973, the *Press-Scimitar*'s Robert Johnson described it as "an unusual new restaurant," which contained "shades of the past [blended] with imaginative planning for a warm, elegant, informal Victorian atmosphere in which hand-carved woods and one-hundred-year-old stained glass set the scene." Despite the high-toned atmosphere, Fisher made sure to emphasize that the Public Eye was a barbecue restaurant by having a forty-three-thousand-pound double barbecue pit in the middle of the restaurant. In the fall of 1974, the Public Eye began offering live blues music on the weekends, and many celebrated musicians, including Furry Lewis, Bukka White, Piano Red Williams and Little Laura Dukes, performed there, making it as much a night spot as a barbecue place. A few years later, Donald Pelts and David Sorin bought the restaurant. Pelts managed it until the early 1980s, when he sold his interest to Sorin. In 1994, Sorin sold the business to Alan, Hal and Mitch Goldberg, who closed the restaurant in July 2000.

After the closing of the Public Eye, Pelts laid plans to open a barbecue restaurant in East Memphis, far away from the working-class neighborhoods that invented Memphis's signature food. "There was great barbecue in the 'hood,' but people wouldn't go there for dinner," explained Pelts's son, Barry.

The Public Eye was a popular barbecue restaurant in Memphis during the 1970s and 1980s. *Courtesy of the Memphis and Shelby County Room, Memphis Public Libraries.*

This must have come as a surprise to the hundreds of Memphians who ate barbecue in the so-called hood. As a fan of the 1981 hit movie *Porky's*, Pelts planned to use that name for his restaurant until a copyright holder prevented him from using the brand. The restaurant was then christened Corky's, which opened at 5259 Poplar Avenue, near White Station, in 1984.

Business grew steadily, and Corky's eventually partnered with FedEx to ship barbecue across the United states. Corky's sold frozen pork shoulder and ribs to 1,500 grocery stores located throughout the country, and in the early twenty-first century, their barbecue was sold on a home shopping TV channel. In May 2003, Corky's ribs and pulled pork were the daily special value on the QVC Network—3 slabs of ribs were being sold for $62. During the sale, which lasted for twenty-four hours, QVC sold 7,000 slabs per hour for a total of 126,000 slabs of ribs and 275,000 pounds of pork valued at $1.57 million. When writer and filmmaker Lolis Eric Elie was researching his 1996 book *Smokestack Lightning: Adventures in the Heart of Barbecue Country*, he visited Corky's and later wrote:

> *It is immediately apparent that Corky's has a very different mission from the traditional barbecue joint. It is not after truck-drivers and tour buses: it is catering to a distinctly middle-class, relatively sophisticated customer who, were he to tire of the long wait for a table that is the norm here, would probably not go to another barbecue restaurant.*

PAYNE'S, THE COZY CORNER AND NEELY'S

While the Peltses were reaching out to the so-called better element, three restaurants were maintaining barbecue's relationship with the poorer neighborhoods of Memphis. Emily Payne and her son, Horton, opened Payne's Barbecue in 1972 on Lamar, near Barksdale. Writing in the *New York Times*, the poet Richard Tillinghast urged his readers to order a "hot brown on bread." He said, "You'll be served the crispiest, juiciest pulled barbecue pork shoulder in Memphis, served on Wonder bread with hot sauce made from vinegar, red peppers and black pepper, with a finely chopped coleslaw that tastes of hot mustard and sugar."

In 1977, Raymond Robinson opened the Cozy Corner on North Parkway, near Danny Thomas and the Hernando Desoto Bridge. In addition to ribs and pulled pork, Robinson offered smoked bologna and barbecued Cornish hen.

Even after the Cozy Corner was celebrated in the *New York Times* and became a local and tourist favorite, Robinson and his grandson, Bobby Bradley, never gave up on the surrounding neighborhood. "It used to be the freaking ghetto…and a lot of kids from there would come here and order food. Some of them come back to visit and talk about my granddad. Some of them, he impacted their lives in a good way, whether it was a piece of advice or whatever. There's danger everywhere, but we've been blessed in this neighborhood," explained Bradley.

When Jim Neely graduated from high school, he joined the U.S. Air Force and was stationed in California. After he was discharged, he briefly returned to his hometown before starting a successful insurance business back in California. In 1972, he relocated his business to Memphis, and a few years later, he purchased a piece of property on South Third Street that contained a liquor store, a beer joint and a grocery store so that his son, Kelvin, who was disabled while serving in the navy, could have something to do. Neely explained: "At the time I came here, it was probably one of the roughest corners anywhere in a major city in America." His response was simple: if someone got out of line, he pulled a pistol and told them, "I don't believe in calling the police. I call paramedics." His wife, Barbara, was also known to "throw men out with a billy club." In 1979, Neely closed the businesses and opened Interstate Bar-B-Q after building his own pit and seeking advice from Brady Vincent. Like Payne's and Cozy Corner, Interstate became a popular restaurant without giving up its neighborhood roots. As the Cozy Corner's Bobby Bradley declared, "I never want to get to the point that people say, 'Don't go there, it's too touristy.'"

THE BARBECUE CAPITAL OF THE WORLD

The success of Jim Neely, Raymond Robinson and Emily Payne came at a time when Memphis was being celebrated for its pulled pork culture—so much so that Memphis proclaimed itself the barbecue capital of the world in 1979. Much of this attention came as a result of a month-long festival called Memphis in May. Founded in 1977 to honor a different country each year, Memphis in May hoped to bring international business to the Bluff City. In the festival's first year, events were held across the city, but most had little or nothing to do with the culture and history of Memphis. So, the following year the city held a barbecue competition, which, a couple of years later, became the Memphis International Barbecue Cooking Contest.

In the competition's first year, 1978, 26 teams competed for a $500 cash prize, and it was won by Bessie Louise Cathey. In 1981, 180 teams entered the contest, and, by 2018, 250 teams from around the world competed for prizes. The contest has also drawn a number of celebrities—the first being writer Calvin Trillin, who wrote a long essay for the *New Yorker* magazine in 1985. After describing Memphis as "a place where an extra ion of American ingenuity might be hanging in the air," Trillin wrote that "the immediate popularity of the barbecue contest was a sign that some civic nerve had been struck—that what people in Memphis had been wanting to do all those years was not to watch a banker dressed up as a king but just to walk along next to the river and sniff the aroma of pork ribs being exposed to a hickory-wood fire."

The contest did more than attract cooks and celebrities—it also expanded the barbecue restaurant business. Corky's, Cozy Corner, Payne's and the Rendezvous all benefitted from the added attention that the contest brought to pulled pork. In addition, several contestants parlayed their award-winning entries into opening their own restaurants. In the early 1980s, John Willingham opened a barbecue restaurant in the suburb of Collierville and constructed a pellet-fed rotisserie cooker that he patented under the name W'ham Turbo Cooker. In 1983 and 1984, Willingham won first place in the ribs competition and was awarded the grand championship. After that, he expanded his restaurant into several locations, but, like Little Pigs, Loeb's and Gridley's, Willingham's World Champion Bar-B-Que grew too fast, and he eventually had to file for bankruptcy. Craig Blondis and Roger Sapp competed in the Memphis in May contest, and from there, they opened Central Barbecue at 2249 Central Avenue in 2002.

Barbecue eating establishments are at the core of Memphis's restaurant history. As Richard Tillinghast wrote in the *New York Times*: "Almost anywhere in Memphis, you can catch an appetite-whetting whiff of hickory-smoke, peppery sauce and ribs or pork shoulder slowly roasting over charcoal. With 62 places to eat barbecue, this sprawling old city overlooking the Mississippi River takes its favorite cuisine very seriously." Singer Wendy Rene agreed; in her 1964 Stax Records release, "Bar-B-Q," she sang: "Here comes pop from up the street and he's got some barbecue. All the kids are startin' to pat their feet because they want some barbecue."

4
"Memphis Is a Meat and Potatoes Town"

When World War II ended in 1945, there were over six hundred restaurants operating in the Bluff City. These included Addie Mae's Eat Shoppe at 303 Monroe Avenue, Dutch Boy Cafe on 576 North Second Street and the Inderbitzen's Lunch Room located at 1269 Latham Street. Popular African American restaurants included the Harlem Cafe at 311½ Beale Street, owned by Vashli and L.M. Howell, and Hawkins Grill at 1251 East Mclemore Avenue, owned by Emmett and Warren Eva Hawkins.

THE MASTER TODDLE HOUSE

When we last visited Toddle House, in 1940, the company had just opened its 101ˢᵗ restaurant at 1703 Union Avenue. Toddle House restaurants continued to open during World War II, and, in 1947, there were 169 Toddle House restaurants in 82 major cities, including Boston, Dallas, Raleigh, New York and Minneapolis. In December 1947, the Master Toddle House—which contained forty seats as opposed to the regular ten—was opened at Third Street and Madison Avenue, where the original Jim's Place was located. Designed to be a training and equipment testing center, the Master restaurant contained "conduction cookers" that were capable of frying bacon in thirty seconds. The restaurant also contained double coffee urns, scrambled egg mixers, hot plates and a soda fountain. The counters were made of stainless steel, the floors were tiled, the stools were upholstered with green leather and the walls were made of glazed tile. All of this decoration came together to give the Master Toddle House a clean and sterile atmosphere. Above the counter were recessed lights with smoky glass transparencies advertising the restaurant's specialties. The Master store had a basement filled with a commissary, where meats and pies were prepared, as well as automatic dish washers and sterilizers.

A few years after the Master Toddle House was opened, the fortunes of the company began to decline. Company president Frederick Smith died in 1949, and founder J.C. Stedman passed in November 1950. Then, in January 1952, the Office of Price Stabilization (OPS) filed a complaint in federal court asking for $88,471 in damages from the Toddle House for increasing prices on ham, pies and hamburgers in violation of government regulations. The investigation surrounding this complaint uncovered further evidence of price manipulation, which led, in March 1952, to a federal indictment of seven Toddle House officers for defrauding the United States government.

Between December 19, 1950, and January 25, 1951, the OPS froze prices to avoid rampant inflation. According to the U.S. government, Toddle House officers conspired to falsify records to reflect that "prices charged and authorized to be charged for various food items…were higher than the prices which were actually charged." A trial was scheduled for June, but the case was apparently settled before then. A decade later, in May 1962, Toddle House was acquired in a $18,278,000 stock transaction by another Memphis-based food service company, Dobbs Houses Inc.

GREEN BEETLE CAFÉ

When Frank J. Liberto was a little boy, he used to sell newspapers in front of a small café called the Green Beetle. Liberto remembered saying, "If I ever grow up, I'm going to run a place called that." True to his word, he opened the first Green Beetle Café in 1933. Several years later, he moved the café to 325 South Main, where he served hotcakes, eggs, bacon and sausage for breakfast, a meat and three vegetables for lunch and a T-bone steak for dinner. By the time World War II began, the Green Beetle was as much a honky-tonk bar as it was a restaurant. Servicemen flocked to the place to drink beer and fight. Liberto explained: "Two shore patrolmen and two policemen [were] paid to stay here, and they still couldn't keep them quiet."

Through the 1950s and 1960s, the reputation of being a rough joint stuck to the Green Beetle even as overt violence declined. Bruce Ebert of the *Commercial Appeal* wrote: "On almost any Saturday, one could find a henpecked husband, a tourist or a prominent businessman sitting at a table or on a barstool, espousing a cure for all that ails the world, or drowning in his tears, or just chatting." In June 1971, Liberto opened the café, but none of his employees showed up for work, so he closed the place. It did not stay shuttered long—several different people owned it through the 1980s. In the 1990s, it became a deli, and in 2006, it reopened as a restaurant whose slogan was "good eatin' like mama's kitchen."

THE CUPBOARD

Bertha Reid opened the Cupboard Tea Room, a small restaurant located in the lobby of the Kimbrough Towers at 1495 Union Avenue, in 1942. It remained a nondescript neighborhood diner until 1992, when Charles Cavallo, a wholesale produce dealer, bought the restaurant for $3,750 in a tax sale. "The Cupboard was always a meat-and-two, or a meat-and-three, place, but I added more dishes that focused on providing the freshest veggies in town," Cavallo stated. In 2000, Cavallo moved the restaurant to a larger location at 1400 Union Avenue, which has become one of the city's most popular gathering places. Indeed, it is not much of an exaggeration to state that if you visit the Cupboard often enough, you can run into nearly every citizen of Memphis. In recent years, Cavallo's sons, Andrew and Jereme, have joined the business and are running much of it. In a 2018 article, Emily Adams Keplinger of the *Commercial Appeal* wrote:

> *Cavallo attributes his ability to grow his business to staying in tune with the world of produce. Dishes such as Italian spinach, fried green tomatoes, corn pudding and eggplant casserole all have their devotees. And as The Cupboard celebrates more than 75 years in business, it is hard to argue with its overall success.*

BUNTYN'S CAFÉ

Located near Highland, at 3070 Southern Avenue, was Buntyn's Café, which was opened in 1927 across the road from the Southern Railroad's Buntyn depot. During World War II, it was owned by Blanche Kampen, and it offered sandwiches, beans, soup and pie for weary passengers making their way to Memphis. After the war ended, Bill Tull bought the restaurant and expanded the menu to include fried chicken and southern-style vegetables. When Tull died in 1964, William B. Williams and his daughter, Betty Wiggins, took over the restaurant. In 1972, Williams passed, and Betty conviced her husband, Milton, to join in the running of Buntyn's. Under Betty and Milton, Buntyn's became a beloved Memphis institution.

In the 1980s, the restaurant served one thousand pounds of fried chicken per week, and, according to reporter Susan Thorp of the *Memphis Business Journal*, the Wigginses' establishment was "known for its homemade rolls, chocolate, lemon and coconut pies, the Buntyn also [dished] out about 420 servings of cobbler every day except Wednesdays, when the fare [was] banana pudding." Like several other Memphis restaurants, Buntyn's had a national reputation. *Cook's Magazine* wrote in 1986: "How about their startlingly juicy fried chicken, its brittle crust impregnated with pepper? We could rave on but let us simply say that if we had to have lunch in one restaurant anywhere in the world…it would be at Buntyn." Four years after the article was printed, Milton passed, and his son, Mike, took over the operation. In 1997, the Memphis Country Club, the owners of the property, refused to renew the Buntyn's lease, and, on March 6, 1998, the restaurant closed its doors. It reopened at Park and Mt. Moriah, but in 2005, they were evicted. Buntyn's Café seemed to be at the end of the line. However, in 2016, Mike Wiggins opened the Buntyn Corner Café at 5050 Poplar Avenue in the Independent Bank Building, where Betty ran the register until her death in 2018.

THE GRIDIRON SYSTEM

In the fall of 1938, a twenty-six-year-old Brooklyn native named Harris Scheuner was hitchhiking through Mississippi when he was picked up by a Memphian. Scheuner had been working as an unsolicited securities trader making $800 a day, but he had recently decided to quit. "Finally, I just couldn't take it any longer. My conscience was hurting me. I made one sale that hurt especially bad. I was disillusioned and wanted to get away," Scheuner remembered. Although Harris Scheuner's pockets were empty, he was wearing a tailored suit and a forty-dollar Stetson hat. His ride took pity on him, and when he dropped him on the outskirts of Memphis, he handed Scheuner twenty-five cents and wished him well.

After spending fifteen cents on beef stew, Scheuner used his remaining dime to pay for a ride to downtown Memphis. Shortly after arriving, he entered a dry goods store owned by Fred Kastleman and boldly asked for a job. Kastleman couldn't understand why someone so well-dressed would want a position that paid only two dollars a day, but he shook off his doubts and offered Scheuner a position as a salesman. After leaving Kastleman's employ, Scheuner briefly owned a liquor store and the East End swimming pool before purchasing the Madison Avenue Gridiron Restaurant from Lawrence "Buster" Levy in 1943. Labor shortages plagued the restaurant at first. Scheuner recalled, "I washed dishes and peeled potatoes when we couldn't get help." However, the wartime economy soon boomed, and he had enough capital to open additional restaurants. In 1944, Scheuner scoured the streets of Memphis, looking for appropriate locations. "We had to find spots with heavy pedestrian traffic," explained Scheuner.

In order to expand, Scheuner had to get around the wartime federal ban on new building construction, so he purchased prefabricated buildings and had them shipped to Memphis on railcars from all over the country. By early 1945, he had opened six additional restaurants and formed Gridiron System Inc. to oversee the twenty-four-hour restaurants. Later that year, Scheuner's company bought the struggling Cotton Boll Restaurant on East Parkway for $20,000—an investment he made back in less than a year. The Cotton Boll continued to be successful until the 1960s, when the State of Tennessee forced the Scheuner family to sell the property for a proposed interstate highway through midtown's Overton Park that was never built. Next, Scheuner acquired the Tennessee Hotel Café, which was very popular with local musicians since it was open late. Up to this point, the Gridiron System had experienced one success after another, but things quickly changed when the company opened the Gay Main, named for Gayoso and Main Streets, at 470 North Watkins across the street from Sears Crosstown. "We had beautiful walls—clean, shining. It was as efficient as you could get….Brother, that was a stinker. Those walls were efficient, but they just didn't make the food taste good," Scheuner explained to a newspaper reporter in 1951.

Although the Gay Main failed as a restaurant, the owner, Harris Scheuner, was able to salvage part of the neon sign for his Gay Hawk drive-in. *Courtesy of the Memphis and Shelby County Room, Memphis Public Libraries.*

While he pondered what to do with the Gay Main, Scheuner focused his attention on a set of customers that were largely ignored by white businessmen: African Americans in Memphis. In 1952, WDIA, the first radio station in the United States to adopt an all-black format, commissioned a survey to discover the buying power of African Americans in Memphis. The survey found that black Memphians accounted for 38 percent of all department store sales and that over half the community's population owned their own home. Realizing that this was an untapped market, Scheuner opened several Harlem House restaurants that were segregated versions of his Gridiron shops: "There, we gave them cleanliness and a place they could buy milk shakes."

Scheuner also knew that a third of Memphis cars were registered to African Americans, which led him to open a drive-in tailored to black automobile owners called the Gay Hawk. Scheuner chose the name so that he could salvage the $3,000 neon sign he used for the failed Gay Main. Designed like a ranch house and equipped with air conditioning, the Gay Hawk became known as a decent place to eat and hear music. At first, the restaurant relied on jukeboxes to provide music to dance and eat to: "A fellow comes in alone. He puts in a nickel, picks out his record and he's got company," Scheuner said. Later, however, the Gay Hawk became a mecca for African American musicians.

According to the "International Queen of the Blues," Toni Green: "In my early days, I was at the Gay Hawk all the time. Back in the day, when black performers were booked at places like the Gay Hawk, that's all we had." Memphis's first African American mayor, W.W. Herenton, echoed Green when he stated: "Gay Hawk was a drive-in restaurant where those blacks who were fortunate enough to have an automobile would go to socialize and take the ladies and style. It was the place to go." One Memphian who hung out at the Gay Hawk was Lewis Bobo Jr., who first visited the drive-in in 1951: "I rode over here with three other guys my first time. I thought it was such a nice place." Bobo was particularly impressed that a white person was responsible for creating the Gay Hawk. "He was the only [white man] who came forward and put up a nice restaurant that was decent."

In addition to the Gay Hawk, Scheuner opened the Harbor Restaurant on the site of the Gay Main in 1951. An important piece of the Gridiron System was its centralized food preparation and supply chain operations. Forty-five employees worked in the office located at 711 South Dudley

Harris Scheuner's Harlem House restaurants catered to African American customers. This one was located on Beale Street. *Courtesy of the Memphis and Shelby County Room, Memphis Public Libraries.*

BOBO'S GAY HAWK RESTAURANT
Specializing in
Steaks — Chops — Seafood — Southern Fried Chicken — Beverages
Complete Catering Service
Open 9 a. m. until ------------------- 7 Days a Week
685 South Wellington   525-9726

The Gay Hawk was Memphis's first drive-in for African Americans. *Courtesy of the Memphis and Shelby County Room, Memphis Public Libraries.*

Street. They operated a bakery that produced all of their hamburger buns, pies and other bread products while a different plant created fifty thousand gallons of ice cream and machines sliced and diced vegetables, which were then delivered to each restaurant. Scheuner and his company also purchased whole carcasses of meat instead of buying small cuts in bulk. Three hundred employees worked in all of the restaurants, where, each month, they fed the equivalent of the entire Memphis population.

The same year the Gay Hawk and Harbor opened, the Gridiron System Inc. grossed over $2 million in profits. In 1954, Scheuner spent $50,000 remodeling the old One Minute Café on Beale Street and called it the Country Club Restaurant. Located between the New Daisy and the Palace at 328 Beale Street, the twenty-four-hour restaurant was managed by John W. Lacy, the former supervisor of the Southern Cooking School. "I don't think there's anything in the South for Negroes which can compare with the new Country Club," Lacy proudly explained.

Despite this overwhelming success, Scheuner was a troubled man. In the summer of 1959, he had trouble sleeping and was suffering from an ear infection, which led to spells of dizziness. Fearing that his health was deteriorating, Scheuner took drastic action. On the evening of July 13, he sat in his office on Dudley, pulled a .38 Colt revolver from his desk, put the barrel to his right temple and pulled the trigger. He was only forty-six years old. After Scheuner's tragic death, company operations fell to his widow, Fannie Katzerman, and their son, Joe. They continued to operate the Gridiron and Harbor restaurants, but, in 1961, they closed the Gay Hawk. Mrs. Scheuner approached Bobo, who agreed to reopen the restaurant and finance the purchase of the restaurant, which was completed in 1977. Lewis Bobo Jr. died in April 2018, and his daughter, Terica, continues to operate the historic restaurant. The Harbor was eventually closed, and Joe Scheuner sold the Gridiron Restaurant chain in September 1996.

WILMOTH'S

In 1942, Charles W. Wilmoth, a restless high school dropout, opened a small café at 714 South Dudley Street, near Elmwood Cemetery. For over a decade, he operated restaurants in several locations across Memphis until 1958, when he opened Wilmoth's Cafeteria at 2265 Park Avenue, near Airways Boulevard. Four years later, Wilmoth opened a second cafeteria at 1985 South Third Street, in the Southgate shopping center. According to the *Press-Scimitar* newspaper, a Wilmoth "customer is faced with a modernistic building of imaginative design.…The interior is as attractive as the exterior; subdued lighting, muted colors, fixtures of graceful simplicity; an atmosphere of quiet spaciousness." Wilmoth explained to the reporter: "We don't go in for exotic foods. Memphis is a meat and potatoes town and has been for a long time." Some of the non-exotic fare available at Wilmoth's included broiled steak, fried chicken and strawberry pie. When the South Third location opened, the response was so great that Wilmoth was forced to hire additional staff to meet customer demand. In 1966, he opened a third location at 3110 South Perkins Road in Parkway Village, which soon became his most profitable location. As a result, Wilmoth sold the South Third location to Don H. Robbins and the Park Avenue restaurant to William O. Dixon in the early 1970s. As a member of the Tennessee Restaurant Association, Wilmoth was elected president in 1964 and was later inducted into the association's hall of fame. Wilmoth continued to operate the South Perkins location until he sold it to Dixon and retired in 1993.

DOBBS HOUSES INC.

James K. Dobbs Sr. quit the fifth grade in his hometown of Fort Payne, Alabama, to get rich quick. He worked as a novelties salesman in Birmingham and St. Louis before coming to Memphis, where he sold cars at the Union Motor Company owned by John T. Fisher. Partnering with former city engineer Horace Hull in 1921, Dobbs borrowed $20,000 from Fisher to purchase a Ford dealership in Memphis. The two made a successful team—Dobbs, the restless salesman, and Hull, the realistic manager—and they quickly turned Hull-Dobbs into a multimillion-dollar business with franchises in thirty-one cities across the United States. In 1939, Hull-Dobbs became the world's largest Ford Motor Company dealership—a title it held for over twenty years.

Always looking for the next opportunity, Dobbs hit upon his next business venture during a turbulent plane ride in 1941. The stewardess became terribly air sick and was unable to feed the passengers, so Dobbs volunteered to serve the cold box lunches. When the flight was over, Dobbs couldn't stop thinking about the terrible meals he had passed out. From that one bumpy experience, the auto dealer formed Dobbs House Inc., which he built into the nation's largest aircraft catering business before it branched out to airport coffee shops.

When Dobbs passed in 1960, his son, James Jr., was named president, and he expanded their restaurant holdings. In 1962, they merged with Toddle House, and by 1964, Dobbs owned 502 Toddle House restaurants across the country in addition to 14 airport snack bars and 66 restaurants that were under the Dobbs House name. To adequately supply and control the consistency of these far-flung establishments, Dobbs House opened a commissary, test kitchen and training school at 3771 Airways Boulevard, near the Memphis International Airport. The commissary delivered 120 dozen eggs, 1,400 steakburgers, 140 pounds of sausage and 120 pounds of coffee per day. In addition, the commissary made 73,000 pounds of dehydrated potatoes, 54,750 pies and 182,500 sweet rolls per year. On June 30, 1966, Dobbs House merged with Beech-Nut Life-Savers Inc., and in the 1970s, they opened 260 Steak 'n Egg Kitchens in Memphis and across the United States. These restaurants were similar in concept to the Gridiron restaurants. Even with its merger with Beech-Nut, Dobbs House remained a primarily Memphis-based company until it was sold to Carson Pirie Scott & Company of Chicago in 1980.

THE KING OF MEMPHIS BISCUITS

Born into a sharecropping family in Lepanto, Arkansas, William Earl Ridling loved his mother's biscuits, and, after serving in the navy during World War II, he borrowed $400 to open a small café on Jefferson Avenue. "My mother was a woman who cooked biscuits three times a day," said Ridling, "and I thought they were good enough to build a restaurant on." He and his wife, Louise, opened the Third Street Café in 1946, and a few years later, they moved the café around the corner to Iowa Street, where they launched Earl's Hot Biscuits. The move to Iowa Avenue (whose name was soon changed to E.H. Crump Boulevard) was a fortunate one. In December 1949, the street was connected to the Memphis and Arkansas Bridge, which meant hundreds of travelers passed by Earl's as they drove east and west across the Mississippi River.

Business increased further when Ridling added a large neon sign of a cook rolling biscuits, which became a well-known landmark until it was replaced in 1977 with another sign that stated: "We Specialize in Country Food, Country Ham & Redeye Gravy." In 1964, a second Earl's Hot Biscuits was opened across the river in West Memphis, Arkansas. Ridling continued to operate both restaurants until he retired in 1982 and closed the original Memphis location. His wife, Louise, and son, Jim, continued to run the West Memphis location until December 1999, when Jim Ridling was injured in a serious automobile accident and forced to close the iconic restaurant. "I had no one to run it. My mother's too old and my wife is taking care of me," Ridling explained. In March 2000, Jim's son, Brad, reopened a version of Earl's next to the courthouse in nearby Marion, Arkansas.

FRIEDEL'S, DAVIS WHITE SPOT AND THE EMBERS

On Poplar Avenue, between Tillman and Holmes Streets, stood Friedel's restaurant—known to many Memphians for the large chef's head sign out front. Born in Memphis, Peter R. Friedel graduated from Central High School and Washington and Lee University before beginning his restaurant career. In addition to his restaurant on Poplar, Friedel also owned the Bavarian Inn and Rescalla before his death in 1967 at the age of fifty-five.

Farther down Poplar, near present-day Estate Drive, stood the Davises' White Spot restaurant. The White Spot was originally a tavern that was opened sometime in the 1930s or 1940s by Ruby Davis and managed by her brother, Robert Winfield. Davis died in 1944, leaving the property to Winfield, which he and his wife, Pearl, converted into a restaurant. According to an early 1940s menu, the White Spot offered sirloin and T-bone steaks for $1.50, fried spring chicken for $1.25, chicken livers on toast for $1.00 and ravioli or spaghetti for $0.35 each. In the 1950s, the Winfields' nephew, Robert Wire, explained to Memphis historian Michael Finger:

> [The restaurant] *was just white wood siding, and the two main dining rooms had knotty-pine paneling. The ambience on the whole was not classy, but very warm and inviting. The parking lot was gravel with a large tree in the center, and the gardens were pretty, with rose bushes and swings and a*

little artificial pond….I have a lot of fond memories of the place, because it was a kid's paradise. I would play in the semi-formal gardens in the daytime, and, in the evenings, I would get to help out in the kitchen.

Davis' White Spot closed when Robert Winfield died in 1961.

Harris Scheuner's brother-in-law, Barney Katzerman, partnered with Harry Glaser to open the Embers at Park Avenue and Getwell Road, in the Park shopping center. Continuing Memphis's reputation as a "meat and potatoes town," the Embers offered roast prime rib, sirloin steak, half spring chicken, hamburger steak, fried chicken and fried shrimp. The steaks were charbroiled and flame-kissed on an open hearth by Chef Eugene Ryan. By the early 1970s, the Embers declined in popularity, and in 1974, Sam Bomarito bought the declining restaurant before it closed the following year.

THE LUAU

During the late 1950s, as Memphians drove or walked past the Dobbs House restaurant on Poplar Avenue, they saw a curious sight. Construction workers redesigned the colonial-style building into something more exotic—a canopy made to look like the prow of a ship that was attached to an exterior shaped like a pagoda. The finishing touch was a replica of one of the famous Easter Island statues. When it was finished in February 1959, citizens learned it was a new restaurant owned by Dobbs House called the Luau. One of the first people to visit the new establishment was *Press-Scimitar* staff writer Mary

The Luau, opened in 1959, was one of the most unusual specialty restaurants in Memphis. *Courtesy of the Memphis and Shelby County Room, Memphis Public Libraries.*

the finest polynesian drinks in Memphis ...or we'll make your favorite beverage the way you like it.

also featuring choice steaks, prime ribs and polynesian entrées

Dobbs House

LUAU

RESTAURANT

3135 POPLAR • PHONE 324-5577

We honor American Express BankAmericard and Master Charge

Allie Taylor, who filed a detailed report describing the new interior: "In the entrance is a waterfall with a banyan tree rising toward the roof, dotted with coral and giant clam shells, with anthurium and birds of paradise... mosquito curtains of bamboo strung with wooden beads partition the entranceway from a lounge lined in tapa of unusual color and furnished with stools and low brass tables."

Customers had the choice of seven different dining areas, including the Firefly Room, where twinkling lights simulated a night in the jungle; the Kamahamaha area, where bows and arrows, spears and war clubs were displayed; and the Sea Gate Room that contained furniture from Hawaii, Hong Kong, Japan and the Philippines. The menu reflected the restaurant's Polynesian theme: char siu, chocho, crab rangoon, Hawaiian barbecued ribs, po po and rumaki. When the Luau opened, it became an immediate hit— high school students especially loved the place and even nicknamed the Easter Island statue the "cool ghoul," which they used as a gathering place. The Luau was also a place where Memphians ate on special occasions, such as birthdays and graduations. Despite its popularity, the Luau became

An advertisement showing the Luau's "Cool Ghoul." *Courtesy of the Memphis and Shelby County Room, Memphis Public Libraries.*

less exotic as more dining options became available in the 1970s. As changes came to Dobbs House in the 1980s, it was decided to do away with themed restaurants like the Luau and instead focus on their Steak 'n Egg and Toddle House enterprises. "The closing is not really a financial matter," explained Dobbs executive Patrick Murphy shortly before the Luau was shuttered in February 1982. "This is simply the end of an era for the Luau."

KNICKERBOCKER

Vernon Bell was an amateur golfer who founded the Memphis Open professional golf tournament, which is now the FedEx–St. Jude Classic. After serving in World War II, Bell bought the Little Tea Shop on Madison Avenue, and in 1954, he built the Knickerbocker Restaurant in a shopping center at Poplar Avenue and Perkins Road in East Memphis. The atmosphere was old English: dark walls, tartan plaids and a hand-painted mural of sailing ships. Managed by Eddins Hops, the Knickerbocker quickly developed a reputation as a restaurant that provided excellent customer service. Bell explained: "You go into a restaurant and get a bad meal; rarely will you get a second chance at that customer. A third time, never. There's where quality and service are important. The atmosphere you create means so much, too. The attention of the employees and their friendliness. You put it all together and that determines your success."

In addition to the Knickerbocker, Bell also owned several Bonanza Steak Houses and a local sandwich chain called Danvers—named for Danny Love, Dan Turley and Bell. For lunch, the Knickerbocker served sandwiches, soups, chicken, pork chops, prime rib and cold platter salads,

Vernon Bell opened the Knickerbocker in 1954. *Courtesy of the Memphis and Shelby County Room, Memphis Public Libraries.*

such as their chicken salad supreme, which contained chicken salad, fresh fruit and Jell-O. The restaurant's dinner menu included oysters Rockefeller, a seafood platter, broiled Spanish mackerel and steaks. Bell sold his Bonanza Steak Houses and Danvers before his death in 1985, and the Knickerbocker closed soon after.

ANDERTON'S

Herb Anderton, born in Memphis in 1914, began his adulthood as a professional boxer. Fighting in matches throughout the South, he fell in love with seafood. He said, "I would always go to the seafood places in New Orleans. I would go back in the kitchen and watch the chef." In 1945, he opened Anderton's Oyster Bar at 151 Madison Avenue in downtown Memphis, which quickly became one of the city's favorite restaurants. It was so well liked that, by 1953, over two million people had eaten there. Oysters were the favored dish, but Anderton's served all types of seafood. Oysters from the Gulf of Mexico were sent to the restaurant daily; the shipments left New Orleans at 11:00 p.m., arrived in Memphis at 6:00 a.m. and were delivered to Anderton's by 8:00 a.m.

In 1956, Herb bought the Gilmore Sea Food Cafe at 1901 Madison Avenue for $40,000 and rechristened it Anderton's East. Four years later, an additional six-thousand-square-foot space was added to the downtown location, which included a large private dining room that seated one hundred customers. For the next decade, both locations remained very popular, but as Memphians abandoned the downtown area in the 1970s, and after Herb's son, Robert, decided to leave the business, Anderton was forced to close the original location in December 1975. However, the midtown location continued to thrive.

In 1980, Robert returned to the business, and, with Herb's granddaughter, Lisa, they oversaw a major expansion of the restaurant, which increased seating capacity to four hundred and added a banquet room. Anderton's lunch menu included baked stuffed deviled crab, fried tenderloin of trout, broiled Spanish mackerel, fried chicken and spaghetti. For dinner, the restaurant offered fried soft-shell crabs, shrimp jambalaya, lobster Newberg, filet mignon, pork chops, liver and baked pompano with crabmeat en papillotte and other seafood entrées, including their famous oysters. In 1987, Herb Anderton died. He was mourned not only for his exceptional food but

RESTAURANT & OYSTER BAR

For the finest sea food anywhere! Specializing in oysters on the half shell, lobster tails . . . 40 varieties of sea foods fresh daily from the Gulf Coast. U.S.D.A. Prime charcoal broiled steaks featured on complete menu. Private rooms available.

151 Madison Ave. • 525-6100 • Also East location—1901 Madison

Herb Anderton fell in love with seafood while traveling through the South as a professional boxer. *Courtesy of the Memphis and Shelby County Room, Memphis Public Libraries.*

also for his support of the University of Memphis and his numerous civic endeavors. Robert continued to operate the restaurant, which remained as popular as when Herb was alive. The restaurant became so well known that it was described as "a venerable seafood establishment called Anderton's" in John Grisham's 1991 best-selling novel *The Firm.* In December 2005, Robert closed Anderton's East before passing away in 2009.

THE BEEF AND LIBERTY

Herb Anderton briefly owned a restaurant in the Whitehaven suburb called Anderton's Oak Acres. In 1967, he sold the property to William M. Tidwell so that he could open a fine-dining establishment called the Beef and Liberty. Located on Highway 51, across the street from Elvis Presley's stately

The Beef and Liberty was located across the street from Elvis Presley's stately home, Graceland. *Courtesy of the Memphis and Shelby County Room, Memphis Public Libraries.*

home Graceland, the Beef and Liberty was based on an eighteenth-century London establishment that was founded by the Gentlemen of the Sublime Society, who pledged to "behave as a worthy member of this society so beef and liberty may be your reward." Tidwell spent $50,000 creating an old English atmosphere with an open-hearth steak broiler, dividers for intimate dining, seating for 250 and cart service. The Beef and Liberty was a popular restaurant until tourists poured into the area after Elvis Presley's death on August 16, 1977. A year after Elvis died, the Beef and Liberty was converted into a gift shop, and Elvis Presley Enterprises bought the property in 1983.

FOUR WAY GRILL

In 1947, Clint Cleaves and his wife, Irene, bought a small café on Mississippi Boulevard, near Walker. They were so determined to own a restaurant that they put their house up for collateral in order to secure a $1,500 loan. Clint was the chauffeur for Memphis political boss E.H. Crump, which left Irene in charge of the Four Way. As she later stated: "We had a signed contract. He would work his job, and I would run the business." Irene was both a good cook and a savvy businessperson—by the 1950s, the Four Way Grill was a beloved institution to the African American community in South Memphis.

Locals were not the only ones who enjoyed Irene Cleaves's cooking and the Four Way's down-home atmosphere. Musicians like Teddy Pendergrass and Gladys Knight ate there, as did Stax artists Isaac Hayes, the Bar-Kays and the Staple Singers. Comedian Redd Foxx visited the Four Way, as did Dr. Martin Luther King Jr. during his early visits to Memphis. Clint passed away in 1979, but Irene continued to serve the people of South Memphis well into the 1990s. In a 1982 review published in the *Commercial Appeal*, the newspaper declared:

> *Four hungry folks visited the grill on a Tuesday and found the lunch menu to include beef hash, fried chicken, salmon croquettes, and chopped sirloin steak. Soul food entrées included boiled chitterlings and pigs' ears....Fried chicken is a favorite at the Four Way, and it is easy to see why. The skin is fried golden crisp while the interior is moist and juicy.*

Three years later, the Reynolds Metals Company honored Irene Cleaves with the Preservation of Black Heritage Award for her contributions to the foodways of Memphis and the South. By the early 1990s, Irene's health deteriorated, and the business fell on hard times. In November 1996, the restaurant fell behind on its taxes, forcing the State of Tennessee to close the Four Way until they could pay $20,000. Recognizing the value of this historic restaurant to the Memphis community, Mayor W.W. Herenton created an advisory committee of representatives from the Four Way, the city and African American business associations. As a result of their efforts, Irene's sister, Bernice Martin, and her son, George, secured a loan from Union Planters Bank and quietly reopened the Four Way in April 1997. A year later, Irene died and the Martins closed the Four Way, but four months later, they sold a ten-year lease to Vernon "Ray" Norment.

Norment reopened the Four Way in February 1999 and ran the restaurant until he filed for bankruptcy in 2000. Willie Earl Bates and Tyrone Burroughs, owners of B&B Associates bought the restaurant and renovated

COMPLIMENTS OF

FOUR WAY GRILL

Mr. and Mrs. Clint Cleaves, Props.
Mrs. Blanche Woods, Manager

1002 Mississippi Avenue   Phone 9-9294

Clint and Irene Cleaves opened the Four Way Grill in 1947. *Courtesy of the Memphis and Shelby County Room, Memphis Public Libraries.*

it in 2002. The Four Way is now an economic anchor for the long-neglected neighborhoods of Mississippi Boulevard and South Memphis. Featured on the Food Network, the Four Way Grill remains a beacon for good food and economic development in a historic part of the Bluff City.

PAPPY & JIMMIE'S LOBSTER SHACK

One of the most colorful characters to ever own a restaurant in Memphis was Lehman Clark Sammons—known to everyone in town as Pappy. Born in Dancyville, Tennessee, in 1879, Pappy came to Memphis at the age of ten to live with relatives. He began his lifelong career as a dishwasher and went to work for "the prince of Memphis Restaurateurs," John Gaston. "That's where I learned what I know today," said Pappy. "In later years, the restaurant business became too commercial, but in that era, it was sentimental." Pappy opened his first restaurant at the corner of Calhoun Avenue and Front Street in 1910, and for the next thirty years, he owned eateries at several downtown locations.

In 1947, he partnered with Jimmie Mounce to open Pappy & Jimmie's Lobster Shack on Madison Avenue, near Cooper Street. The restaurant consisted of four houses that were joined together on the edge of a residential district. Neighbors complained to Memphis political boss E.H. Crump, who, according to Pappy, told the residents, "I've known that man for nearly sixty years, and he runs a high-class place. If he gets out of line, I can take care of that, but, until he does, let's live with him and see how it turns out." Mounce and Pappy opened Pappy & Jimmie's Restaurant at the corner of Poplar Avenue and Hollywood Street in 1952 but dissolved their partnership in 1956—with Pappy keeping the Lobster Shack and Jimmie remaining as owner of the restaurant.

Like so many eateries, the Lobster Shack suffered a devastating fire in 1962, but Pappy reopened and continued to offer excellent food in an atmosphere surrounded by curiosities he had collected, which he referred to simply as "junk." When Pappy celebrated his one hundredth birthday in April 1979, a large celebration was held in his honor. Attendees nibbled on lobster-shaped birthday cake while Congressman Ed Jones read a congratulatory letter from President Jimmy Carter. Unfortunately, Pappy could not come—he was in St. Joseph's Hospital recovering from a viral lung infection. A month later, he was walking through his house to pick up the morning paper when he

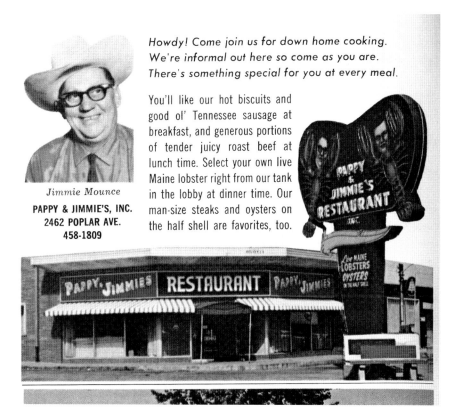

Howdy! Come join us for down home cooking. We're informal out here so come as you are. There's something special for you at every meal.

You'll like our hot biscuits and good ol' Tennessee sausage at breakfast, and generous portions of tender juicy roast beef at lunch time. Select your own live Maine lobster right from our tank in the lobby at dinner time. Our man-size steaks and oysters on the half shell are favorites, too.

Jimmie Mounce

PAPPY & JIMMIE'S, INC.
2462 POPLAR AVE.
458-1809

Pappy & Jimmie's Lobster Shack was owned by one of the most colorful Memphians of the twentieth century, Lehman Clark "Pappy" Sammons. *Courtesy of the Memphis and Shelby County Room, Memphis Public Libraries.*

collapsed and died. Many Memphians mourned the loss of one of the city's greatest restaurateurs, who was a living link to the city's past. As the *Press-Scimitar* stated in an editorial: "He added color and stability to the quality of life in Memphis. He will be hard to replace."

JACK PIRTLE'S

It is obvious that crispy, golden-brown fried chicken has long been a staple of Memphis's diet. One of the most popular fried chicken restaurants in Memphis history was named for its founder and has been shorthand for quality fried chicken for nearly sixty years.

In 1945, Jack Pirtle moved from his hometown of Toone, Tennessee, to Memphis and opened a diner near the Firestone plant in North Memphis. Two years later, Pirtle moved his diner to Linden Circle and christened it the High Hat Café. He later opened a third establishment, the Jefferson Café, in downtown Memphis at the intersection of Third Street and Jefferson Avenue. One day, in early 1957, the café's regular bread delivery driver casually mentioned to Pirtle that his uncle was having a great deal of success selling fried chicken. The driver then offered to introduce him the next time his uncle came to Memphis. A few days later, Pirtle had breakfast with Colonel Harland Sanders, where he asked permission to sell his secret recipe chicken. Scrutinizing the Jefferson Café, Sanders blurted out, "Hell no. You can't sell my chicken in here!" Pirtle didn't give up, and after four days of discussion, Sanders agreed to give him a few boxes of chicken, seasoning mix and a sixteen-quart cooker. Pirtle cooked his first chicken on February 14, 1957, and, before long, it became his most popular item. As Pirtle described in 1981: "We started selling about two cases of chicken a week, and, by the end of four weeks, we were selling all we could cook. By May, I was looking around for a spot just to sell chicken." The spot he eventually chose was 1217 Bellevue, which became Jack Pirtle's Kentucky Fried Chicken.

At first, business was slow-moving; no one in Memphis really knew anything about Kentucky Fried Chicken except that it wasn't from Tennessee. However, once they figured how delicious it was, Pirtle was selling $900 worth of chicken a day. In 1960, he opened a second restaurant on Summer Avenue, and he opened a third at 811 South Highland Street near Park Avenue the following year. The grand opening of this location occurred on November 17 and 18, 1961, with Colonel Sanders himself participating in the festivities. Balloons and recipe books were passed out to the two thousand people who flocked to the drive-in restaurant to enjoy the Colonel's secret recipe. So many came that traffic was backed up on Highland Street, past Southern Avenue, for much of the grand opening weekend. In 1961, you could get enough chicken to feed four to six persons for $3.25, and a snack-sized meal cost $0.65.

Three years later, Pirtle chafed at new regulations from the KFC corporate office, including one that required him to use paper bags instead of boxes for takeout orders. When he refused to comply, Pirtle said, "They gave me thirty days to get rid of everything associated with Kentucky Fried Chicken." He painted all of the stores blue and yellow, bought new cooking equipment, devised his own recipe and reopened the outlets as Jack Pirtle's Fried Chicken. Jack Pirtle passed away on August 5, 1985, but the restaurants that bear his name continue to offer some of the best fried chicken in town.

MAHALIA JACKSON'S GLORI-FRIED CHICKEN

As it has been previously mentioned, segregation limited the opportunities for African Americans to eat at or own restaurants in Memphis. This began to change in March 1960, when a group of students from LeMoyne College and Owen Junior College led a series of sit-in demonstrations at restaurants and lunch counters, as well as public libraries and parks. The sit-ins lasted until November 1961, when the majority of downtown restaurants and lunch counters agreed to desegregate. Three months later, thirty additional Memphis restaurants agreed to desegregate, which prompted the Justice Department to congratulate Memphis for its integration efforts. When legalized segregation was outlawed in the 1964 Civil Rights Act, the movement shifted its attention to issues of economic inequality.

In Memphis, a group of African American leaders, including state representative A.W. Willis and criminal court judge Benjamin L. Hooks,

Gospel singer Mahalia Jackson, seen here with Floyd Newsum, Andrenetta Jones, Benjamin L. Hooks and A. W. Willis, lent her name and reputation to a fried chicken restaurant chain designed to provide business opportunities for African Americans. *Courtesy of the Memphis and Shelby County Room, Memphis Public Libraries.*

met two months after the assassination of Dr. Martin Luther King Jr. to discuss business opportunities for African Americans. The group was aware that the growth of fast food restaurants across the United States largely ignored African American communities. Willis proposed: "A nation-wide fried chicken carry-out franchise system offered the greatest involvement and profit to hundreds of retail outlet owners." Willis, Hooks and the others approached famed gospel singer Mahalia Jackson to ask her to lend her name and reputation to the enterprise, to which she readily agreed. In an interview, Jackson explained: "From a corporate standpoint, we wanted to develop a black-owned, black-staffed, franchise system. Then bring this system into the black community and make franchising opportunities available to the residents of these communities." In order to have enough capital to start the operation, Nashville politician John Jay Hooker, who owned the Minnie Pearl fried chicken restaurants, invested $5 million.

The first Mahalia Jackson's Glori-fried Chicken restaurant opened in September 1969 at 705 South Parkway. The following year, restaurants were opened in Charlotte, Chicago, Cleveland, Detroit, Houston, Jacksonville, Milwaukee, Nashville and the Bahamas. The Detroit restaurant took in $10,000 in sales per week, but by the end of 1969, the company needed more capital to stay afloat. The company hoped to raise $10 million in a public stock sale in which they would sell shares for $10 each—but when the Dow Jones average fell below seven hundred, they postponed the sale. At this time, the Securities and Exchange Commission also began investigating Hooker and his Minnie Pearl restaurants. Mahalia Jackson's restaurants were caught up in the investigation, and when Hooker's company sold their shares in Mahalia Jackson's, the company went under. Neither company was ever charged with wrongdoing, but the SEC investigation, combined with the stock market downturn, forced the Mahalia Jackson Chicken System Inc. into bankruptcy.

HUNGRY FISHERMAN

In November 1972, the company that operated the Shoney's restaurants in Memphis opened the Hungry Fisherman, located on an eleven-acre lot near the edge of the lake on I-40 and Macon Road. The *Press-Scimitar* columnist Robert Johnson visited the restaurant and wrote this description:

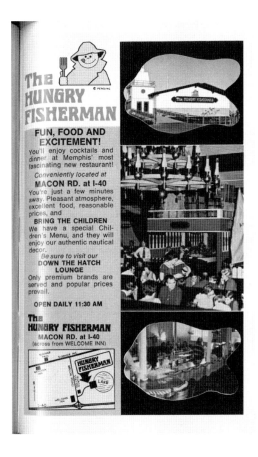

The Hungry Fisherman seafood restaurants were opened in 1972. *Courtesy of the Memphis and Shelby County Room, Memphis Public Libraries.*

You enter the restaurant on a slightly inclined wooden ramp, and the rails at the sides are big oars, authentic even to not having been painted....The restaurant itself, a vast room, has a beautiful chandelier...windows on all sides giving a view of the lake, seats 425....Salad bars, from which patrons serve themselves, are in three lifeboats, with stainless steel receptacles for salad, dressings....On the far wall is the captain's bridge, and an entrance leads to an outside bridge with rail, from which children, and adults, can feed some of the 50,000 fish [with] which the lake will be stocked. The menus are on boards, shaped like a fish. As is to be expected, the emphasis is on fresh fish and seafood.

A second Hungry Fisherman was opened at 350 Goodman Road, near Horn Lake, Mississippi, and the menu at both locations consisted of such items as catfish, red snapper, North Atlantic whitefish, stuffed filet of flounder and Idaho rainbow trout. Perhaps their most popular dishes were the all-you-can-eat selections of calabash shrimp, catfish filet, fried clams, filet of perch and fried chicken. Like the Luau, the Hungry Fisherman was one of the most popular high-concept restaurants to open in Memphis and it remained so until it closed in 1993.

ZINNIE'S

In 1973, Gerry Wynns and a few other investors opened a bar and restaurant at the corner of Madison Avenue and Belvedere Boulevard called Zinnie's. According to the *Commercial Appeal*'s Micaela Watts, Zinnie's was a "longtime hangout for musicians, journalists, college students, people with dirty clothes (the bar conveniently was located across the street from a laundry) and other Midtown habitués, Zinnie's had few windows and a dark, wooden interior that inhibited excess sunlight." Wynns soon bought out the other investors and opened two other locations at 107 South Court and 79 Jefferson Avenues. In the late 1980s, he also built Zinnie's East a few doors down from the original location. When Wynns died in 1994, he left Zinnie's to Bill Baker and Zinnie's East to Perry Hall. Hall closed Zinnie's East in 2011, and in November 2018, Baker unceremoniously closed the original Zinnie's.

MOLLY GONZALES' LA CASITA

Molly Garcia Gonzales came to Memphis from Texas with her parents, Jesus "Jesse" and Lupe Garcia, in the 1930s. They lived on Arkansas Street, and her father made a living working in the cotton fields around West Memphis, Arkansas. Molly trained to be a nurse, but when she couldn't find a job in 1957, she opened Chiquita's Café in West Memphis, Arkansas. She eventually moved to San Jose, California, with her husband, Fred, to practice her original profession. When Fred's health began to fail, Molly left nursing and they returned to Memphis. In 1975, Molly bought an abandoned Toddle House at 1910 Lamar Avenue, and she opened Molly Gonzales' La Casita restaurant. She explained: "I don't cook from the books. I don't open no books. I cook for taste, and my customers tell me they like it." In 1982, Robert Chapman and a group of investors bought into the restaurant with Molly, who continued to cook her own way. Chapman moved the restaurant from

Lamar Avenue to a new location at 2006 Madison Avenue, and he opened a second location on Park Avenue. The Park location was eventually sold to an Italian restaurant, and Molly passed at the age of ninety-five in 1997. To this day, however, the Madison restaurant remains one of Memphis's most popular Mexican food establishments.

HUEY'S

In junior high school, Thomas Boggs played drums with the Cruisers garage band. When he started attending Central High School in 1960, he joined Tommy Burks and the Counts. The Counts were probably the most popular dance band in Memphis during the early 1960s; in 1963, they recorded for American Studios and opened for the Dave Clark Five the following year. Boggs also performed with Flash and the Board of Directors when they opened for Paul Revere and the Raiders. By the early 1970s, Boggs had left the music business to work for the T.G.I. Fridays franchise on Overton Square. In 1975, he managed a bar called Huey's at 1927 Madison Avenue, and two years later, he became a partner in the business. Boggs oversaw the expansion of the bar into a restaurant that specialized in gourmet hamburgers. He worked with the owner of John Gray's Big Star grocery store to develop a ground beef mixture that had the right blend of fat, lean and spices for the world-famous Huey Burgers.

Huey Burgers come with long toothpicks, and when the restaurant first opened, customers often used straws to blow them into the ceiling. This was considered a nuisance until a customer named Craig Love suggested that Boggs leave the toothpicks in the ceiling and, once a year, have people pay two dollars to guess how many there were. As a result of the contest, $20,000 has been raised every year for local charities, including the Church Health Center, Metropolitan Inter-Faith Association and St. Jude Children's Research Hospital.

Huey's is careful to keep its saloon atmosphere—in 1978, *Press-Scimitar* columnist Lucinda Cornelius described Huey's as "that homey little combination of a beer tavern and hamburger joint." In addition to good food, Huey's also provides a showcase for local musicians with their Sunday night concert series. In the 1980s and 1990s, Boggs opened several other Huey's locations around Memphis and in the nearby suburbs. He also became a partner in other local restaurants, including

Folk's Folly, the Half Shell and Tsunami. Before his untimely death at the age of sixty-three in 2008, Boggs reflected on his thirty years in the restaurant business: "There are two key and equal factors in running a restaurant: your product and your employees. If you take care of your employees, they will take care of you."

FROM 1945 TO 1969, MEMPHIS'S restaurant industry experienced tremendous growth—in 1963, local restaurants served 228,000 meals per day, and in 1967, the National Restaurant Association reported: "Memphis restaurants have increased total sales as much as 20 per cent [*sic*] the past two years." In Memphis, 6,300 workers were employed in the restaurant business with an annual payroll of $12,868,000, and in 1969, there were over 850 eating establishments in the Bluff City.

5

"A Different Style of Cooking"

Although Memphis has the reputation of being a meat and potatoes town, it is filled with restaurants that have historically provided more exotic fare. As we have seen, fine dining first appeared in Memphis during the nineteenth century with the opening of Gaston's and Leurmann's restaurants, and in the 1920s Chinese, Italian and Mexican food was served at restaurants and lunch stands across the city. After World War II, fine French dining returned to the Bluff City, and the number of Chinese, Italian and Mexican restaurants increased while other establishments offered German, Greek and Vietnamese cuisine to Memphis's diet.

THE VILLA

Sam's Eat Shop was opened in the 1930s by Sam J. Sciara and his wife, Rose. Born in Memphis, Sciara grew up working with his Sicilian father, Pasquale, who sold fruits and vegetables. After dropping out of high school at the age of sixteen, Sciara used a bicycle to peddle produce to many parts of the city. A few years later, he opened a fruit stand on Main Street that eventually became the Eat Shop. In 1947, the Sciaras opened Sam's Spaghetti Shop on Poplar Avenue, across from the Auditorium. Business was going well until November 1957, when a fire swept through the restaurant, destroying everything Sam and Rose had worked for since the 1930s. The Sciaras refused to give up, and with the help of their family and an insurance claim, Sam and Rose reopened the business with a new name: the Italian Villa.

On opening night, Sciara invited a group of friends to celebrate his new endeavor with a dinner party. Reverend John Donahue of St. Patrick's Catholic Church blessed the restaurant, and attendees included members of the city commission and high-ranking police officers. Fire and police commissioner Claude Armour explained to the press: "[The] last time I saw Sam, he was standing out in the street with big tears rolling down his cheeks while he watched the fire. And, now, he has this fine place." Sam and Rose's son, Pete, served as the maître d', and the menu included meatballs cured in hot olive oil, steaks soaked in marsala wine and pizzas cooked on hot bricks. A few years later, in the early 1960s, Sam and Pete moved the family restaurant to Poplar Avenue and Perkins Road in East Memphis and shortened its name to the Villa. In 1964, a *Commercial Appeal* columnist wrote, "Sam Sciara right now is elated with the success he's meeting with his smorgasbord—with steaks, shrimps, salads, lobster and all that. Several different colorful dining rooms, a charming little bar. He has food of several nations, too." Sam and Pete opened Palazzino's at 6155 Poplar Avenue, and they later opened Café Max with Pete's wife, Mary, and their children, Carl, Sam, Regina and Rose. Sam Sciara died in 1993 and is remembered as a kind man who believed "the secret to every recipe is love and grace."

FOLTZ'S RANCH HOUSE

As World War II ended, Jesse Foltz and his wife opened the Ranch House on Bowen Road, which is just off North Highland Street in the Grahamwood area. Designed to provide a fine-dining experience in the middle of a residential neighborhood, the Ranch House specialized in steaks that were so good cotton and lumber buyers from many nations, international businessmen and government officials from England, Israel, Turkey and several South American countries routinely sang its praises. The owners attributed their success to their marriage of fine dining to a family table atmosphere. "If a guest wanted a second or third helping, he received it," said Mrs. Foltz. When their son, Jesse Jr., moved to California with his wife and Jesse's nine-month-old granddaughter in 1952, the Foltzes decided to close the restaurant.

THE COACH HOUSE

When Confederate soldier Thomas Newton Patton returned to Memphis after serving in the Civil War, he went to work for a river barge company owned by his uncle. In 1877, he built a two-story, red brick, Victorian-style home at 1085 Poplar Avenue. The home remained in the Patton family until 1900, when it was purchased by Russian immigrant and prosperous merchant Samuel Bejach. Later, the residence was purchased by Walter L. Cawthon, who ran an antique shop out of the home. In 1958, Lessie Gates and her son, Percy Bramlett, bought the house and converted it into an elegant restaurant called the Coach House. Gates had managed the Dobbs House Airport Restaurant and owned the Beacon for many years before she established the Coach House.

Opened in September 1958, the Coach House was divided into three spacious dining rooms: the Duchess, the Early American and the Queen's, all of which contained Adam mantel mirrors, crystal chandeliers, red velvet carpets, gold leaf cornices, satin draperies and gold leaf china. In addition to the three large dining rooms, there were six private dining rooms and two parlors that were available for candle-lit dinners. The restaurant also contained a large, bricked-in yard, which was used for outdoor dining in the warmer months. Reviewing the restaurant for the *Press-Scimitar*, Clark Porteous wrote: "The food is fabulous. Bramlett is buying his meat from Chicago. A thick steak was delicious, beautifully served, preceded by shrimp cocktail and a choice of several salads. The price was $3.95. The specialty of the house is an 11-course Coach House dinner, $5, recommended as an eating experience." In the summer of 1964, Gates closed the restaurant and remodeled it as a private club that included a lounge, a room devoted to playing bridge and a swimming pool. When the Coach House reopened, it had over three hundred members, and that number grew larger by the end of the summer. "What has made me particularly happy is that the customers I had at the beginning have stayed with me thru the years," Gates proudly stated in 1964.

On a rainy morning in March 1965, Ruby Earthman arrived at the rear of the Coach House to begin her shift as head cook. When she found the door locked, she waited under a shed for Gates to arrive, but when she didn't, Earthman asked another employee to call Gates's daughter, Kathleen Novell. Mrs. Novell entered the quiet building and found her mother's glasses lying on the floor. When she got farther into the building, she discovered her mother's crumpled body in a rear storeroom.

Pronounced dead at the scene, police found five bullet wounds in Mrs. Gates's chest, stomach and chin. Two weeks later, Percy Bramlett reopened the establishment, but it was soon inundated with curiosity seekers who only wanted to see a murder scene.

By early May, the situation became so distressing for the family that it was decided to close the restaurant and sell the property. As one family member explained: "We feel a restaurant should be a happy place. It's not a happy place when people just come in to see the family and the place where it happened." Later that year, Al and Mary Sullivan bought the property, and, in October 1965, they opened the Sullivan House. The menu of the Sullivan House included lobster thermidor and shrimp and crabmeat baked in a sea shell. The Sullivans changed the menu and décor of the restaurant, but they were unable to make the Sullivan House a success. The restaurant officially closed in the spring of 1966.

THE FOUR FLAMES

In June 1966, Harlon Fields, the owner of the Flame Room in the Downtowner Motel, received a phone call from Sullivan asking if he was interested in buying his restaurant. Fields was looking to build another establishment but was not interested in that location. He was even quoted as saying, "Man, I wouldn't have that thing." He did, however, agree to look over the place. Fields later said, "I went over there, and my imagination began to work. An hour after I walked in, I bought it." Paying $50,000, Fields named the restaurant the Four Flames after its four flambéed desserts: baked Alaska, bananas Foster, cherries jubilee and peach Melba. Outside the historic structure, Fields placed four white columns with gas flames to identify the restaurant. "We have not put up a sign. We feel we have a perpetual sign in our Four Flames that announces our presence better than neon," explained Fields.

The service at the Four Flames was superb. According to *Press-Scimitar* staff writer Bill E. Burk: "When you walk in, one man seats you at the table, one pours your water, and another brings you butter, another the menu and it goes that way all night." Guests were provided complimentary barbecued oysters, and the menu consisted of entrées such as chateaubriand, flaming tenderloin, flounder Florentine and charbroiled red snapper. By the 1970s, the Four Flames was one of the most respected restaurants in the city. It was

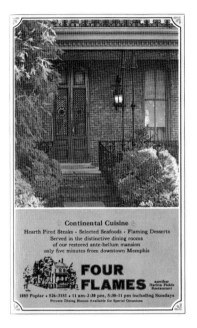

Continental Cuisine
Hearth Fired Steaks • Selected Seafoods • Flaming Desserts
Served in the distinctive dining rooms
of our restored ante-bellum mansion
only five minutes from downtown Memphis

FOUR
FLAMES
another
Harlon Fields
Restaurant
1885 Poplar • 526-3181 • 11 am-2:30 pm, 5:30-11 pm including Sundays
Private Dining Rooms Available for Special Occasions

In 1966, Harlon Fields opened the Four Flames in the location that once housed Lessie Gates's Coach House restaurant. *Courtesy of the Memphis and Shelby County Room, Memphis Public Libraries.*

praised for, in the words of the *Commercial Appeal*, using "its Southern setting and Southern atmosphere to provide authentic Southern hospitality."

In August 1979, the Four Flames was listed in the National Register of Historic Places. However, the economic recession and double-digit interest rates of the late 1970s and early 1980s began to affect the restaurant's operation. United American Bank began foreclosure proceedings against the Four Flames, and in 1983, Fields filed for Chapter Eleven bankruptcy protection. That summer, Fields sold the Four Flames to Hal and Jeannie Brinkley, who were also forced to file bankruptcy in 1987, because they owed United American Bank more than $330,000. Memphis Heritage, the city's historic preservation organization, lobbied the city and state to save the historical building. The State of Tennessee provided the City of Memphis with $328,000 to purchase the home. The city then leased the home to the Memphis and Shelby County Child Abuse Council and Memphis Heritage for $1 a year. Today, it is the home of the Child Advocacy Center.

JUSTINE'S

In the late 1940s, Justine Smith was dissatisfied with the lack of French cuisine available in Memphis restaurants. She discussed her idea of opening a fine restaurant with several friends, including Frank Schutt, who managed the Peabody Hotel, and they all told her she'd go broke. Smith, however, persisted in opening an elegant restaurant in an old warehouse on Walnut Street, next to the Memphis Street Railway's bus barn. Without any advertising, Smith opened her eponymous restaurant in 1948. On the first night, it was so crowded that Smith's friend, Frank Schutt, was unable to secure a table. Meanwhile, Dayton Smith, Justine's husband, renovated a nineteenth-century mansion at 919 Coward Place, where they moved Justine's in 1956. Their French cuisine with a dash of New Orleans flavor included entrées like filet de boeuf béarnaise, oeuf Sardou, pompano à la claudet, and crab Florentine.

Three of the greatest American writers, who would often visit Memphis, made their way to Justine's. Nobel Laureate William Faulkner and his daughter, Jill, ate there whenever she returned home from school, and Civil War historian and novelist Shelby Foote was the first person to open a charge account at the restaurant. Pulitzer Prize–winning playwright Tennessee Williams would also take his grandfather there to celebrate his birthdays.

Between 1956 and 1970, Justine's was celebrated as one of the nation's finest restaurants by *Holiday*, a well-known travel magazine. "An exquisite garden, continental cuisine combined with the best of regional cooking have earned this award from the country's most respected—and trusted—source," wrote the magazine's editor. On New Year's Eve in 1995, Justine's long tenure as one of America's most celebrated restaurants came to a close. Justine explained her retirement by saying, "Forty-eight years is a long time. It's a very nostalgic time, and I hate to do it, but I need to have some life by myself."

PAULETTE'S

The 1956 anti-Communist Hungarian Revolution led to one of Memphis's most iconic restaurants. Archaeologist Paulette Fono and her husband, Laszlo, a physical education teacher, fled Hungary just before the Soviet Union invaded and crushed the nascent revolution. After relocating to the United States, they both worked in a bank in Denver for several years before opening a restaurant called the Magic Pan. After successfully operating three Magic Pan Restaurants in Denver, Quaker Oats bought controlling interest in the company and opened locations in Aspen, Atlanta, Chicago, New York and San Francisco. Placed on the board of directors, Laszlo and Paulette were disgusted by how the parent organization operated their restaurants. As Paulette described it: "We couldn't believe it. They didn't place any emphasis on the quality of the food and service in the restaurants. All they cared about [were] the bottom-line profits."

In 1974, George Falls convinced Lazlo and Paulette Fono to open a French restaurant in Memphis. *Courtesy of the Memphis and Shelby County Room, Memphis Public Libraries.*

In 1968, they met a Memphian named George Falls, the vice president of international franchising at the Holiday Inn motel corporation, who asked them to consider establishing a restaurant in Memphis. "He kept telling us that most of the restaurants in Memphis served only a steak and salad type of menu. He told us he wanted [us] to come to Memphis so that he could enjoy a different style of cooking," explained Paulette. With the financial backing of Falls, the Fonos opened Paulette's on Madison Avenue, in the Overton Square entertainment district, in 1974. Four months later, they opened a similar restaurant in San Francisco, but they traveled to Memphis often to oversee Paulette's. Five years later, Falls and two partners bought the restaurant from Laszlo and Paulette, and in 1984, George Falls became the sole owner. Paulette's menu consisted of house specialties, including broccoli fromage, veal ragout, brochettes of lamb, ham palacsinta, spinach crêpes and crêpes à la bretonne.

Falls closed Paulette's Overton Square location in February 2011, and he relocated it to an upscale neighborhood on Mud Island, a subcontinental strip of land connected to Memphis by a bridge.

ERIKA'S

In addition to restaurants that served great Chinese, French, Mexican and Italian cuisines, Memphis was home to a restaurant that served exceptional German food. Erika Seipel was born in Frankfurt, Germany, where she learned to cook at a trade school. While working at a department store, she met a Memphian by the name of W.W. Seipel, who was visiting his sister in Frankfurt. The two eventually married and settled in the Bluff City, and in 1977, they opened Erika's German Restaurant at 52 South Second Street with their partner and fellow German immigrant Mady Smythe. Erika declared in 1980: "All of our food is made here at Erika's, and I do most of it myself. What cooking I don't do—I supervise." Her lunch menu included German sausages like bratwurst, knackwurst, bockwurst and munchner weisswurst served with potato salad or sauerkraut, and her dinner menu contained jagerschnitzel, kassler rippchen, leberknodel, sauerbraten and weiner schnitzel. Erika and Mady continued to serve German food until they quietly closed the restaurant in April 2006. As their faithful customer Jim Baymiller wrote: "How I will miss her schnitzels, pan fries, red cabbage, spaetzle, yeast rolls, goulash suppe and Black Forest cake!"

COLETTA'S

Born in Italy, Emil Coletta served as a sergeant in the Turkish-Italian War of 1911, and during the First World War, he served as a lieutenant and was shot in the chest by a German soldier wielding a machine gun. Two years after the war ended, Coletta immigrated to the United States and settled in Memphis, where he opened the Suburban Ice Cream Company at 1063 South Parkway East in 1922. "He had sandwiches and spaghetti back then, and he had an ice cream wagon drawn by a horse. But, the main attraction was restaurant-made ice cream," his grandson Jerry Coletta stated. In addition to his ice cream company, Emil was very active in Italian American civic organizations. In 1939, for example, he was elected commander of the Italian World War veterans. His ice cream business was very popular, but by the 1940s, when his son, Horest, joined the business, his Italian cuisine was bringing more people to the restaurant, especially soldiers stationed in Memphis who routinely traveled down South Parkway while out on a pass.

you'll enjoy
tranquil dining
in an atmosphere
of OLD ITALY

Coletta's
FINE ITALIAN FOODS

- 4940 SUMMER AVE.
  Opp. Holiday Inn

- 1063 S. PARKWAY E.
  WH 6-9163

Horest Colletta created the barbeque pizza, which remains a local sensation. *Courtesy of the Memphis and Shelby County Room, Memphis Public Libraries.*

Memphians loved Emil's spaghetti, but there was one thing missing from the menu: pizza. According to Horest, "[I] had come from the east where they had pizzas, but pizzas weren't available in Memphis, so I asked my father to show me how to make pizzas, and we started." As the Colettas' pizza grew in popularity, they had a decision to make—"Were we going to be an ice cream business or were we going to be a restaurant?" asked Horest. They decided to focus on becoming a restaurant, and, in 1951, the business was expanded and the name was changed to Coletta's Italian Restaurant. Horest took over the business, and he noticed that, despite the popularity of their pizza, many Memphians refused to try it. To entice them, Horest created a barbecue pizza, which soon became a local sensation. Elvis Presley loved eating barbecue pizza and celebrity chef Bobby Flay featured Coletta's and their famous creation on his Food Network TV show *FoodNation*. In 1958, a second Coletta's was opened on Summer Avenue, and it remained in operation until it burned down in 1996. Two years later, Jerry Coletta opened another restaurant near the suburb of Bartlett on Appling Road, and it was run by his three children, Stephen, Kristina Holland and Lisa Morgan. The original South Parkway East location remains popular for those looking for an authentic Memphis dining experience.

GRISANTI'S

Like the Colettas, the Grisanti family has also produced several generations of Memphis restaurateurs. The patriarch, Rinaldo "Willie" Grisanti, emigrated from the Italian town of Valdotavvo to Memphis in 1903. He worked as barkeeper and butcher until he saved enough money to open his first restaurant at South Main Street and Talbot Avenue in 1913. He later opened Willie's Grill on Main Street, and it was there that the Grisantis first became a celebrated Memphis family. According to Rinaldo's oldest son, John: "The food service business on Main Street was not what it is today. It was incidental to bootlegging whisky and policy games. My daddy did all that, sold policy tickets. One time, we almost lost everything because Mama picked the wrong numbers." The policy racket was an illegal lottery that was popular in Memphis during the first half of the twentieth century.

The name of Willie's Grill was eventually changed to Grisanti's, and John entered the family business in 1954, after serving in the military. John remembered how things were when he joined the restaurant: "We only seated 87 and the turnover was great. We served breakfast, lunch and dinner. Daddy worked all day, taking a nap in the middle....I ran the front end and they ran the kitchen." After suffering through two fires at the Main Street location, Rinaldo leased the historic home, Ashlar Hall, and opened the new Grisanti's on Central Avenue near Lamar Avenue. John's brother, Elfo, worked in the kitchen with their parents until their mother, Mary, died in November 1961. John then decided to go out on his own. In 1962, he opened John A. Grisanti's Restaurant at 1489 Airways Boulevard, which had once been the location of the restaurant Pete and Sam's. His menu included several Italian dishes, including polpetti alla caruso—which consists of veal slices stuffed with filling that are cooked in beef broth and risotto Milanese—and Italian sausage and chicken gizzards simmered in chicken broth. Rinaldo passed in 1966, and he is remembered by one of his customers as the most genial man you could ever know. He loved people, and he served good food.

After Rinaldo's death, his son, John, continued to flourish on Airways Boulevard. He became a respected wine connoisseur and was called one of the country's best wine collectors by *Town & Country* magazine. He was named restaurateur of the year by the wine tasting club Les Amis du Vin in 1982, and in 1991, the *Wine Spectator* honored his restaurant with a best-of-excellence award. Fondly known as Big John, he appeared often on local television and was beloved for his kind, outgoing nature. Twice, he bought rare bottles of vintage wine and auctioned off glasses of it to raise funds for St. Jude Children's Hospital. For his civic activities, John was named the Optimist Club's Citizen of the Year, and in 1989, he was appointed a Knight in the Order of Merit of the Italian Republic. Big John died in 1995, and he is remembered as one of Memphis's leading citizens. "He put Memphis

In this 1977 advertisement, John Grisanti, his son John Jr. and his nephew Ronnie are pictured in the kitchen of the Airways Boulevard restaurant. *Courtesy of the Memphis and Shelby County Room, Memphis Public Libraries.*

John Grisanti, seen here with St. Jude Children's Research Hospital founder Danny Thomas, auctioned off glasses of vintage wine to raise money for the hospital. *Courtesy of the Memphis and Shelby County Room, Memphis Public Libraries.*

LOST RESTAURANTS OF MEMPHIS

on the map in wine and food circles…and for his gifts to the community," said wine consultant Shields Hood. His sons, John Jr. and David, ran the restaurant until Big John's wife, Dolores, sold the property in June 1995. As she explained: "I have done this with mixed emotions, but John was Airways, and he's no longer here."

John's nephew, Rinaldo, nicknamed "Ronnie," worked for several years as the kitchen manager of the Airways restaurant until 1979, when he opened his own establishment, Rinaldo Grisanti and Sons. Located at 710 Union and Marshall Avenues, he was joined in the business by his sons, Deano, Judd and Alex. In 1986, Ronnie renovated the buildings that once contained Epstein's Loan Office and Morris Lipman's pawn shop on Beale Street and relocated his restaurant there. Two years later, he closed the Beale Street restaurant and moved to 2855 and 6150 Poplar Avenue. In June 2017, Ronnie Grisanti died and his son Judd took over the business. Writing on his restaurant's website, Judd declared:

> *Now that I am privileged to become a guardian of a more than century old culinary tradition, I make it my mission to create "Antico Nuovo" dishes for your delight in our beautiful dining room. I aim to maintain Italian standards of excellence while bringing my signature and more modern contributions to the Grisanti culinary heritage.*

GIOVANNI'S

The Cerritos were another family who brought fine Italian dining to Memphis. In the 1940s, John Joseph Cerrito opened Cerrito's at Second Street and Washington Avenue. A move to 282 North Cleveland in the Crosstown neighborhood led to renaming the restaurant Giovanni's. Known for its catchphrase, "Where Italy comes to your table," Cerrito resisted attempts to "Americanize" his dishes. The cannelloni, fettucine, lasagna, linguini, manicotti and scampi were prepared with traditional recipes, which made them spicier than those served at other Memphis Italian restaurants. A fire gutted the restaurant in 1983, but the Cerrito family refused to abandon their business. John's son, Rudy, who had recently become a co-owner, declared: "We're third-generation, and we're not going anywhere. I don't plan on quitting feeding people in Memphis now."

The Cerrito family operated Giovanni's Italian restaurant on Second Street during the 1940s. *Courtesy of the Memphis and Shelby County Room, Memphis Public Libraries.*

Giovanni's was one of Memphis's most popular Italian restaurants until it closed in the 1990s. *Courtesy of the Memphis and Shelby County Room, Memphis Public Libraries.*

True to their word, they soon reopened, and five years later, John retired. Rudy moved the restaurant to 4972 Park Avenue in East Memphis in 1995, and a year later, John passed. The Cleveland location was scheduled to close the evening of February 14, 1995, but so many customers wanted to have one last Valentine's dinner at Giovanni's that Rudy postponed the move by two weeks in order to accommodate everyone. Rudy's wife, Rita, said, "We've had hundreds of phone calls, way past what we could get in. We don't want to leave on a bad note." The move to Park Avenue did not last long, and Rudy unexpectedly died of cancer at the age of fifty-one. Rudy David Cerrito was mourned by many across Memphis. Named chef of the year in 1987 and 1988 by the Greater Memphis Chefs Association, Rudy was a committed volunteer who raised money for United Cerebral Palsy of the mid-South and was given the Daily Point of Light Award by President George H.W. Bush. "It's a loss to the Italian community and to the restaurant community," said Ronnie Grisanti. His sister Toni Jo Cerrito echoed Grisanti's sentiments when she said, "He was very serious about being a chef and to helping others."

PETE & SAM'S

The fourth major Italian restaurant to open its doors after World War II was named for two cousins: Pete Romeo and Sam Bomarito. When Sam got out of the army in 1946, he worked several jobs, but he was really looking for an opportunity to own a business. "One day, my cousin and I were driving down Airways Boulevard, which then was a little narrow two-lane road. I saw this building at Alcy and Airways, and I said to Pete, 'That would make a fine restaurant,'" Sam explained. Neither man had any restaurant experience, but Sam's mother, Rose, taught him how to cook. Each man borrowed $1,800 from their family members and opened Pete and Sam's in 1948. Business was slow; on the first night, they made a grand total of $3. Within a short time, Pete became so bored with the business that he wanted out. He told his business partner, "Sammy, I'm gonna have to leave. I can't stand any more of this."

With Pete gone, Sam ran the restaurant by himself. When a customer arrived, he would seat them and take their order. Then, in order to maintain the fiction that others were working in the back, Sam would call out the order before running into the kitchen to prepare the food. He briefly moved the restaurant to Lamar Avenue and Airways Boulevard, but in 1960, he moved Pete and Sam's to 3886 Park Avenue, where it remains to this day. As he did in so many of Memphis's classic restaurants, Elvis would sneak in and eat in the back room, while entertainer Danny Thomas, founder of St. Jude's Children's Research Hospital, insisted on being served barbecue bologna, even though it wasn't on the menu. Sam served traditional Italian food alongside beef tenderloin and filet mignon—their specialty, however, was their thin-crust pizza.

In the 1970s, Sam bought the Travelin' Fox nightclub, the Knights Out Lounge, the Embers restaurant and a second Pete & Sam's location in the Trave-Lodge near the International Airport—but it was the Park Avenue location that Memphians flocked to. Over the decades, Pete and Sam's developed perhaps the most loyal following of any restaurant in the city. Sam's sister, Vita B. Gattuso, stated: "Most of the people that we know that come in here, we've known them for years and they come up to us and they hug us and they kiss us and they tell us how much they love us." According to longtime customer Anne Hill: "When you go there, you just get the feeling that it's just Memphis, really a part of the city. When you go there, you know you're in Memphis." Sam Bomarito continued to operate Pete and Sam's until his death on March 17, 2012. Now, his sons, Sam Jr. and Michael, continue to run the restaurant that is a Memphis institution.

PANCHO'S

In addition to Italian cuisine, Mexican food became popular in Memphis in the 1950s and 1960s. Traveling salesman Morris Berger and his wife, Clemmye, opened a nightclub called the Plantation Inn across the river at

Pancho's opened a chain of taco shops, including this shop on Summer Avenue. *Courtesy of the Memphis and Shelby County Room, Memphis Public Libraries.*

Morris and Clemmye Berger opened their first Memphis Pancho's Mexican Restaurant in 1960. *Courtesy of the Memphis and Shelby County Room, Memphis Public Libraries.*

West Memphis, Arkansas, in the 1940s. When their son, Louis Jack Berger, graduated from Christian Brother High School in 1951, the family took a vacation to Mexico, where they fell in love with the food. They recruited a Mexican cook named Della Gonzales to come to Memphis, and a few years later, they opened a small Mexican restaurant in West Memphis called Pancho's. When it burned down a few years later, they closed the Plantation Inn and built a new Pancho's on the property. In 1960, the Berger family opened a second restaurant at 1676 Bellevue Boulevard, and by the end of the decade, Pancho's was the most popular Mexican restaurant in Memphis.

A third restaurant was opened at the corner of Union and McLean in 1972, and not long after, several Pancho's fast food taco shops were built on Elvis Presley Boulevard, Walker Avenue, Poplar Avenue, South Perkins and Old Summer Roads. Louis took over the family business after his father's death and expanded the company to include a line of Mexican foods available in grocery stores—including its signature cheese dip. When *Memphis Flyer* writers Michael Donahue and Susan Ellis asked a grocery manager in 2018 what Pancho's cheese dip meant to his business, he replied: "Are you kidding me? It's right behind milk." Louis continued to operate the family business until his untimely death at the age of sixty in 1993. When he passed, the Hispanic population of Memphis was growing dramatically—so much so that the number of Mexican restaurants also expanded to feed this new population. The competition from these new Mexican restaurants forced Brenda Berger O'Brian, who took over the business after her brother's death, to make some hard choices. The fast food taco shops were closed, as well as the original Memphis and Union Avenue locations. In 1982, O'Brian purchased a restaurant site in the Cloverleaf shopping center at Summer Avenue and White Station Road. This location, along with the West Memphis restaurant, are the only locations that still remain. Despite this retrenchment, Pancho's has a very loyal customer base that loves their traditional Tex-Mex dishes.

LA FONDA

Not all Mexican restaurants were as popular as Pancho's. One such establishment was La Fonda, which was created by Clyde McCoy, a trumpet player who often performed at the Peabody Skyway and whose recording of "Sugar Blues" sold millions of copies. In 1965, McCoy, his wife, Maxine, and her brothers, Allin and Frank Means, collaborated to open a Mexican restaurant called La Fonda. The restaurant was located at 2220 Union Avenue in an old home that was redesigned by Allin Means and Maxine McCoy. La Fonda contained four dining rooms that were each decorated with paintings of Mexican street scenes and named for the Mexican cities of Acapulco, Mexicali, Monterrey and Tampico. When the restaurant opened, business was slow, and it never really picked up. This was largely due Pancho's success in the small market that existed for Mexican food in Memphis. In the summer of 1967, the McCoys hired a Mexican chef and troubadours to serenade guests with traditional Spanish music. Business did increase slightly, but by the end of the year, McCoy and his partners closed the restaurant.

JOY YOUNG

Wong Shing Kuel was born in Canton, China, in 1927. After immigrating to Birmingham, Alabama, Wong worked as a cook until he joined the navy at the end of World War II. After serving in the galley of the USS *Fullam*, Wong returned to Alabama and married May Yee Wai Oi in Hong Kong in 1948. The following year, the Wong family moved to Memphis and Wong Shing Kuel changed his name to Jack Wong. In 1952, he opened a Chinese restaurant called Joy Young in the Downtowner Motor Inn, which was located at Union Avenue and Third Street. Wong opened a second Joy Young at 1517 Union Avenue in 1961, which solidified his restaurants' status as having the best Chinese cuisine in Memphis. When the Union location opened, the *Press-Scimitar* stated that the restaurant contained "gentle Oriental pastels of chalk blue and soft rose, grass cloth walls, charcoal wall prints, quiet music…and excellent Chinese and American food." Wong explained: "[The] quiet feeling is important in a restaurant. This is part of the dream restaurant, which came to me many years ago."

In the summer of 1964, John Knott, author of the *Commercial Appeal*'s nightlife column wrote, "Jack Wong's pork fried rice with shrimp and lobster sauce is so good it's downright sinful." Wong eventually opened another restaurant in the Eastgate shopping center, where his egg rolls and pressed duck were popular items on the menu. "Joy" was the perfect word to

Jack Wong opened his first Joy Young Chinese restaurant in 1952. *Courtesy of the Memphis and Shelby County Room, Memphis Public Libraries.*

describe Jack Wong—an outgoing person who loved serving his customers quality Chinese dishes that made him a celebrity in the Bluff City. As Kevin Robbins of the *Commercial Appeal* wrote when Wong died in October 1996: "His name was as synonymous with fine Chinese dining as his Maine lobster Cantonese was with the best dishes in Memphis."

BERNARD CHANG

Born in China, Bernard Chang grew up in Taipei, where his mother taught him recipes that she had learned from her brother, who served as a chef for the Qing Dynasty. In 1970, Chang left Taipei and settled in Memphis, where he worked as an accountant. He had fond memories of his uncle's restaurant in Taiwan, so, in 1979, he opened Ming House on Winchester Road in southeast Memphis. In addition to operating Ming House, Chang also taught Chinese cooking classes, and in October 1983, he started a new restaurant on Beale Street called Kublai Khan. The menu at Kublai Khan contained dishes based on the spicier Hunan, Shanghai and Szechuan styles of Chinese cooking. Two years later, Chang opened a similar restaurant called Genghis Khan at 4698 Spottswood Avenue. A second Genghis Khan soon followed in Clark Tower, and in the early 1990s, he opened China Grill on Overton Square.

Chang was a celebrated chef whom the *Commercial Appeal* described in this way: "What he means to Chinese food is what Pavarotti means to Opera." In February 1995, Chang was severely wounded after he was repeatedly stabbed and left for dead by an angry employee. While Chang recuperated in the hospital, many of the city's most respected chefs volunteered their time to keep the restaurant open, but after four months, the Chang family closed China Grill on June 27. At first, it appeared that Chang would recover, but he took a sudden turn for the worse and died in late July. Bernard Chang is remembered for his culinary skills, and Chef Michael Cahhal spoke for many when he said, "Bernard, as a Chinese chef, was very innovative. He tried to bring together the flavors of the East and the West." Like Jack Wong, Lau C. Chu, Wong Kop and Lee Yett, Bernard Chang contributed greatly to the Chinese community in Memphis while he also expanded opportunities for Memphians to enjoy the full range of Chinese cuisine.

FOLK'S FOLLY

Humphrey E. Folk Jr. and Pete Aviotti opened Folk's Folly, a gourmet steak restaurant, in 1977. *Courtesy of the Memphis and Shelby County Room, Memphis Public Libraries.*

Before entering the restaurant business, Humphrey E. Folk Jr. owned a company that specialized in river construction. Founded in 1967, the company constructed a navigation channel on the Tennessee-Tombigbee Waterway and a levee on the Mississippi River. In the mid-1970s, Folk was approached by two local businessmen, who asked him to finance a restaurant venture. Eventually, the two abandoned the idea, but, by then, Folk was very interested in the restaurant business. During a visit to Nashville, he was sitting in his hotel room with Memphis real estate developer Pete Aviotti, when he asked, "Pete, where do you go and eat steaks in Memphis?" Aviotti replied that there were no good steak restaurants in Memphis. "What would you think if we opened a steakhouse in Memphis?"

In 1977, the two opened Folk's Folly, which was named because Folk thought it might be a folly for a construction man to run a restaurant. Modeled on Chris' Steakhouse in New Orleans, Folk's Folly quickly became the most successful steak restaurant in the Bluff City. Humphrey Folk died in 2004, but his so-called folly remains a prime destination for Memphians hungering for gourmet steak.

THE LOTUS AND MINH CHAU

In March 1975, Joe and Hanh Bach left Saigon—one month before the North Vietnamese Army conquered its southern neighbor. After an arduous journey, the couple landed at a refugee center in Fort Chaffee, Arkansas, where Joe worked as a translator assisting other Vietnamese during their relocation process. A few years later, Joe and Hanh moved to Memphis, where, in 1981, they opened a restaurant on Summer Avenue called the Lotus. They named the restaurant after this flower because it symbolizes family and loyalty. Hanh's mother worked as a private cook for a French family in Saigon, and it was from her that she learned to create such dishes as duck stuffed with chestnuts, garlic, ground chicken, kidney beans, olives, onions, parsley and pork. With their children, Bernard, Han, Kimberly, Solomon and Victor, Joe and Hanh patiently introduced Vietnamese cuisine to a people who were mostly used to plain food. "In the beginning, my parents had a very hard time. People only knew dishes like sweet and sour pork, so my mother had to mix in Cantonese," remembered Han.

Two years after the Bach family left Saigon, Thom Thi Bach (no relation) placed her ten children in a small boat, and together, they slowly floated away from Vietnam. Four days later, they arrived in Malaysia, where Catholic Charities helped them relocate to the United States. A professional egg roll maker, Mrs. Bach cooked and sold egg rolls out of her apartment in Midtown when she arrived in Memphis in 1978. In addition, a nearby bar and restaurant on Madison Avenue called Fantasia added her egg rolls to its menu. Cooking restaurant food in a private home was against Health Department rules, so her operation was shut down in the spring of 1980.

Commercial Appeal reporter William Thomas wrote a story about Mrs. Bach that was read by Kenny Hamilton, owner of the Daily Planet Bar on Park Avenue. Hamilton allowed Mrs. Bach to use his kitchen to prepare her Vietnamese egg rolls before transporting them to her customers. This didn't satisfy the Health Department, which declared that she would have to pay for a $150 food processing license, cook in a kitchen with three sinks and transport the egg rolls in a refrigerated truck. Meanwhile, William Thomas ridiculed the Health Department in a series of follow-up articles. "The plot in the Vietnamese egg roll story thickens: Yesterday, if you remember, it looked like Mrs. Thom Thi Bach, a Vietnamese refugee, would get to make her egg rolls right here in barbecue city and earn some extra money for herself and her 10 children," wrote the *Commercial Appeal* reporter. The newspaper was soon joined by the Memphis Area Chamber of Commerce in opposition to the Health Department's position. The pressure eventually became too great for T.A. Taylor, manager of the environmental sanitation section, who told Thomas that he didn't "want to comment further because it's being taken out of context." Taylor said, "I feel like the more I say, the closer I'm getting to the Mississippi River."

At a contentious hearing, it was pointed out that hot tamale stands and popcorn machines were not subject to these regulations, and Hamilton declared "this hearing has nothing to do with food sanitation—this is a bunch of red tape." The Health Department finally agreed to allow Mrs. Bach to prepare her egg rolls in the restaurants where they were served, as long as she submitted to two health inspections. As William Thomas explained, "Although the Health Department already has spent more time on Mrs. Bach's egg rolls than it normally does on a dozen big restaurants, the health department…made arrangements to watch Mrs. Bach work twice in one day—a highly unusual procedure, according to restaurant people." After passing both examinations, Mrs. Bach was allowed to prepare her egg rolls and sell them at Fantasia and the Daily Planet. With the money she made, Mrs. Bach was able, in 1982, to open the Indochina Restaurant in the Cooper-Young neighborhood. Several years later, she opened Minh Chau on Madison Avenue near Cleveland Street, which, like the Lotus, brought Vietnamese cuisine to the people of Memphis

In a review for the *Commercial Appeal*, food critic Frederic Koeppel wrote:

> *Any meal at Minh Chau must begin with the egg rolls, but a viable alternative is the shrimp rolls, in which translucent, fleshy rice wrappers enclose three or four bright pink shrimp—right under the skin, as it were—and deeper layers of herbs and vegetables spiked on a green onion stalk. We also enjoyed the Vietnamese pancake, a wide swath of deeply browned rice flour and eggs enclosing shrimp, chunks of pork, bean sprouts and other vegetables; eat this with the accompanying lettuce and mint and a ruby-colored, slightly sweet sauce.*

In 1988, Women of Achievement honored Thom Thi Bach as a woman who "seized the opportunity to use her talents and created her own future."

LA TOURELLE AND AUBERGINE

French cuisine was also well represented by two significant restaurants: La Tourelle and Aubergine. In the 1970s, Glenn Hays, the track coach at Memphis State University (now the University of Memphis), spent his summers traveling through Europe, where he became fascinated with continental food. After taking a French cooking course at the university, he and his wife, Martha, partnered with Zinnie's restaurant in 1974 to prepare French cuisine every Sunday afternoon. As Hays said at the time: "There is really nothing in Memphis that serves the type of food you get in a European restaurant." In 1977, they opened their own restaurant, La Tourelle, at 2146 Monroe Avenue near Overton Square. Their opening menu included quiche

Lorraine and beef bourguignon, but the offerings changed every month. For June 1983, La Tourelle offered tournedos charcutiere, red snapper hollandaise, chicken and Roquefort and veal piccatta. Before the restaurant closed in July 2007, La Tourelle employed several important chefs, including Stan Gibson, Erling Jensen and Cullen Kent.

Another noted chef who worked at La Tourelle was Gene Bjorklund, who, with his wife, Juliana, opened Aubergine in 1993. The lunch menu at the East Memphis restaurant included osso buco and mushroom pasta, the most popular item for dinner was their lobster and white bean salad and, for dessert, the restaurant's signature dish was Bjorklund's roasted bananas with passion fruit coulis and white pepper ice cream. In 1998, *Commercial Appeal* dining critic Fredric Koeppel named Aubergine the best restaurant in Memphis, writing: "Gene Bjorklund's food, French in origin, expansive in execution, doesn't overwhelm with incessant richness, though it teems with flavor. His conceptions are daring yet respectful, complex but never fussy." Despite this success, Aubergine closed in 2002.

CHEZ PHILLIPE AND JOSE GUTIERREZ

Historically, the Peabody Hotel was considered the center of culinary arts in Memphis. However, in 1973, it closed, and two years later, it was sold at auction on the courthouse steps. After it was purchased by Philip and Jack Belz, the hotel was completely renovated. When the Peabody reopened in September 1981, it included the fine dining restaurant, Chez Phillipe. The Belz family hired a young chef from Provence, France, named Jose Gutierrez to operate the new restaurant. A graduate of the Professional Culinary School at Manosque, France, Gutierrez trained with such celebrated French chefs as Paul Bocuse, Roger Petit and Francis Trocelier. He quickly turned Chez Phillipe into a nationally known restaurant and became one of the country's most respected chefs. In 1990, he was named America's Best New Chef by *Food and Wine Magazine*, and he was designated a Master Chef of France in 1995. Two years later, he received the Ivy Award from *Restaurant & Institution Magazine*. As Jeffrey Dunham, the president of the Memphis Restaurant Association in 2005 remarked: "Jose put Chez Phillipe and Memphis on the culinary map....He has done a huge amount for the culinary scene in this town."

One of his greatest culinary successes came in February 1998, when the Peabody celebrated the 126th anniversary of Grand Duke Alexei's visit to

Memphis by honoring his direct descendent, Prince Nikita Romanov. The dinner was prepared by Gutierrez, who replicated the eleven-course meal that was served to Alexei in 1872, which included the signature dish: venison with cranberry sauce. After twenty-two years at Chez Phillipe, Gutierrez opened his own restaurant, called Encore, in 2005, which he described as "a bistro, with food from France and Spain and Italy, simple food, not too expensive." Five years later, he became the chef at River Oaks Restaurant, located at 5871 Poplar Avenue, which he and his wife, Colleen, soon purchased. It is easy to come to the conclusion that Jose Gutierrez did the same for Memphis cuisine in the late twentieth and early twenty-first centuries that John Gaston did in the late nineteenth and early twentieth centuries.

IN TWO HUNDRED YEARS, MEMPHIS grew from a town with a frontier cuisine of wild game that was served in rough surroundings to a meat and potatoes town whose many innovations in the preparation of pulled pork contributed greatly to the development of American cuisine. In addition to barbecue, Memphis is also home to a diverse set of restaurants that serve excellent Chinese, French, German, Greek, Mexican, Italian and Vietnamese foods. Taken together, the melding of African, Asian, European, Mediterranean and North American culinary traditions has made Memphis one of the most important culinary cities in the United States.

Bibliography

Primary Sources

The Memphis and Shelby County Room of the Memphis Public Libraries includes in its collection the Memphis Information File, which contains newspaper clippings and other small items organized by subject. This collection includes information on general subjects, like barbecue and restaurants, as well as individual files on the establishments that appear in this book and biographical clippings on many of the restaurateurs who operated in Memphis. Other important sources are the Memphis City Directories from 1850 to the present. Other primary sources include:

A.W. Willis Collection, Memphis and Shelby County Room, Memphis Public Libraries.

Gayoso House Collection, Memphis and Shelby County Room, Memphis Public Libraries.

Fredric Koeppel Restaurant and Menu Collection, Dig Memphis, Memphis and Shelby County Room, Memphis Public Libraries. www. memphislibrary.contentdm.oclc.org.

Secondary Sources

Anonymous. *Memphis Menus: A Collection of Menus from Memphis' Finer Restaurants*. Memphis: n.p., 1982.

———. *Memphis Menus: The Most Complete Collection of Menus from Memphis' Finer Restaurants*. Memphis: n.p., 1983.

Bateman, Joy. *The Art of Dining in Memphis 2*. Memphis: J. Bateman, 2011.

Grisanti, John. *Wining and Dining with John Grisanti*. Memphis: Wimmer Brothers, 1984.

Lauderdale, Vance. *Ask Vance*. Memphis: Bluff City Books, 2003.

———. *Ask Vance, Book Two*. Memphis: Contemporary Media Inc., 2011.

Lolis, Eric Elie. *Smokestack Lightning: Adventures in the Heart of Barbecue Country*. New York: Farrar, Straus and Giroux, 1995.

Meek, Craig David. *Memphis Barbecue: A Succulent History of Smoke, Sauce & Soul*. Charleston, SC: The History Press, 2014.

Rodack, Jaine. *The Peabody: A History of the South's Grand Hotel*. Memphis: Peabody Publication, 2007.

Smith, Janet Stuart. *Justine's: Memories & Recipes*. Memphis: Wimmer Companies, 1998.

Stewart-Howard, Stephanie. *Barbecue Lovers Memphis and Tennessee Styles*. London: Globe Pequot, 2015.

Wells, Carolyn. *Barbecue Greats: Memphis Style*. North Kansas City, MO: Pig Out Productions, 1991.

About the Author

G. WAYNE DOWDY IS THE senior manager of the Memphis Public Library's history department. He holds a master's degree in history from the University of Arkansas and is a certified archives manager. Dowdy is a contributing writer for the *Best Times* magazine and *Storyboard Memphis.* He is the author of *A Brief History of Memphis*, *Hidden History of Memphis* and *On This Day in Memphis History*, which was awarded a Certificate of Merit by the Tennessee Historical Commission.

Visit us at
www.historypress.com
....